# HOW TO
# TALK TO
# PORCUPINES

A Youth Worker's
Communication
Field Guide

## Allegra Birdseye-Hannula

BEAVER'S
POND
PRESS

Porcupine illustrations and icons courtesy of AKimball Creative, LLC
Book design and typesetting by Dan Pitts

ISBN 13: 978-1-64343-702-6
Library of Congress Catalog Number: 2022911443
Printed in Canada
First Edition: 2024
27 26 25 24 23    5 4 3 2 1

 Beaver's Pond Press
939 West Seventh Street
Saint Paul, MN 55102
(952) 829-8818
www.BeaversPondPress.com

To order, and to get exclusive content, join the community, and expand your prickly porcupine tool kit, visit howtotalktoporcupines.com.

Contact the author at howtotalktoporcupines.com or howtotalktoporcupines@gmail.com for school visits, speaking engagements, and interviews.

Learn more on Facebook (@howtotalktoporcupines), Instagram (@howtotalktoporcupines), or LinkedIn (linkedin.com/company/howtotalktoporcupines).

*To the strong, powerful matriarchs in my family who put up with
a lot of prickly porcupines and extended opportunities to us all
in hopes of creating a better world*

*And to my spouse . . . who puts up with my own occasional quills*

# Contents

# Using This Guide

Youth have unique stories to tell, and prickly personalities (*porcupines*) share their stories to express a need. It is important to help unlock and hear the porcupine's story to address the need. But quills hurt—especially when they get under your skin. This guide is designed to give you environmental cues, tips, and tricks to respond appropriately when prickly personalities arise.

Youth workers encounter porcupines often, and the need to deal with prickly situations is a common occurrence. **Communication** breakdowns are often at the heart of those challenges. Unless you learn to quickly defuse and de-escalate these situations, your program outcomes may be at risk. Learning how to break down communication barriers will help you better understand and engage with the young people you serve.

Youth work is a vast, diverse, and ever-changing field. Youth workers include teachers, after-school or summer program staff, early-childhood staff, educators, program or guidance counselors, school resource officers, nurses or physicians, peer and adult mentors, youth leaders, youth programming managers, coaches, community officers . . . the list goes on. If you work with youth on a regular basis, you are a youth worker, and this book is for you.

Each section includes a Take Action activity designed to help you apply your learnings and develop your own action plan for redirecting and de-escalating porcupines. Study this guide independently; read it with a learning buddy to take action alongside; or even use it as a team to establish your own collective communication strategies. A full version of the Field Guide Workbook is available in the appendix so you can return to your action plan and make modifications as you grow in your field.

I hope you find this guide an informative, practical resource to which you can refer over and over throughout your career.

# What This Guide Is Not

This guide is intended to provide you with tools for face-to-face conversations during which your safety is not threatened. This guide is not a tool for

- de-escalating dangerous or violent situations;
- replacing your existing mediation, de-escalation, or trauma-informed strategies; or
- addressing specific segments of behavioral or mental health challenges, including but not limited to oppositional defiance disorder (ODD), autism, bipolar, schizophrenia, or addiction.

Know your limits, acknowledge your training, and be aware of when you need to bring in resources with more formalized training. Think wisely and exercise your judgment when working with prickly porcupines.

The information in this guide is intended as a supplemental resource. It is not meant to replace proper training and education in medical, mental health, psychology, psychiatry, or emergency response. Recognize when you feel seriously unsafe or threatened, and first seek to remove yourself from the situation. Then take a deep breath and assess whether you need to call in backup. Your physical safety is important. The safety of the youth in your care is important. Know your limits.

# My Youth Work Story

I did not wake up one day and proclaim my desire to become a youth worker. I fell into the career through a series of stepping-stones and a calling to serve our next generation.

In preschool, I wanted to be a firefighter, then an astronaut. Then I wanted to be a kid for the rest of my life (this should have been my first sign). As I reflect, however, I now realize helping others has been a staple of my identity since childhood.

In elementary school, I volunteered as a reading mentor. Weekly, I met up with my "book buddy"—a student several years younger than I—to pore over books together on the dusty hallway floor. As a teenager, I helped lead team-building and life skill activities as a mentor and peer counselor in my church's youth group during summer camp. I helped freshmen transition from middle school to high school as a peer mentor. I also helped youth hone their own communication skills to compete in mock trial and forensic (speech and debate) tournaments at the local, state, and national level. At the local Boys & Girls Club, I dove into more formalized youth work as a lifeguard, coordinating water activities for neighborhood youth.

At the time, these were just activities. I entered college firmly believing I would graduate to become an attorney or a press secretary or a speechwriter for influential politicians . . . but, as it does for many college students, life pushed me in a different direction. I ended up gravitating toward youth work.

As part of my college work-study program, I ran after-school programming for students in southern Minnesota. I tutored a middle school student in ESL when I studied abroad in southern China, approximately 7,487 miles from my home. I returned home to lead summer programming activities for youth living in a transitional housing complex.

After graduating, I moved to the Twin Cities and landed a job coordinating evening tutoring activities for an inner-city homeless shelter. Some of my favorite memories come from leading art, education, and cooking activities for youth at the shelter. I have coached high school forensics, taught financial literacy, and earned my secondary social studies teaching license. Each step or role has reinforced my passion for serving youth.

My youth work journey has informed my own communication style and helped me build out my communication tool kit to effectively communicate with porcupines. Today, I share my experiences and best practices with other youth workers through virtual and in-person training opportunities. This book is inspired by lessons learned from all the prickly porcupines I've encountered over the years. Through it, I hope to share my learnings through research, evidence-based practices, and personal experiences in an accessible field guide workbook.

Happy trails!

*Allegra Birdseye-Hannula*
*she/her/hers*

# Prickly Personalities

## Identification: Porcupine

**Latin:** *porcus* (**pig**) + *spina* (**spine, prickle**)
**Common:** porcupine, quill pig, prickly hog, spiny pig

To effectively communicate with porcupines, we must first identify what porcupines are, how they show up, and when they might appear.

A porcupine is a large nocturnal rodent that may appear in various shades of brown, gray, or white. More than two dozen species exist across Africa, Asia, Europe, North America, and South America.

## FUN FACT
A group of porcupines is called a *prickle*.

Although porcupines may den together during the winter months, they prefer independent autonomy. Very resourceful creatures, porcupines use their quills, tail, and hind legs to propel themselves up tree trunks or climb large branches to find food.

Porcupines often chatter their teeth to warn predators not to approach. When frightened, a porcupine quickly becomes prickly and defensive. It might turn its back toward the predator and raise its quills as a final warning. If ignored, the porcupine may whack the predator with its tail or a well-placed pawful of quills. These sharp quills contain barbs (overlapping scales), making them very difficult to remove once stuck.

## FUN FACT

I learned about the danger porcupine quills could pose when I was very young because they were often used in artwork and clothing by artists in my school and community. As a child, I had an unfounded fear of porcupines because I thought they could "shoot" their quills. As an adult, I now know that's just an old myth.

Like porcupines, youth desire independence and autonomy to make their own decisions. They are resourceful and employ warning systems to alert others to back away or change course when threatened or challenged. These warning systems serve as a means of self-preservation to ward off perceived conflict or to help the youth meet an unmet need.

## TAKE ACTION: BRISTLY BEHAVIOR

*Write your answer here or in appendix 1, section 1.*

Porcupines demonstrate warning behaviors to predators. What behaviors do youth demonstrate when threatened, fearful, or concerned for their safety?

# Field Study: Tru

*Tru came to my tutoring and activities program fifteen minutes late, just shy of the program cutoff. He was paired with a volunteer tutor, who eagerly began talking to him.*

*A few moments later, the volunteer approached me for help: Tru was not responding to questions or participating in the assigned activities. I walked over, greeted Tru, and asked how he was doing. Tru placed his head on the table and closed his eyes. I had just encountered a porcupine.*

*The volunteer tutor and I saw a withdrawn, disinterested youth who refused to participate. This was not uncommon—youth frequently leveraged tactics to get out of tutoring and focus on computer time, crafts, or games instead.*

*What we didn't know was that Tru had just gotten off his school bus after a two-hour commute. He had missed mealtime and was still processing the experience. I learned this additional context when I contacted his parent to explain the situation. We resolved the communication impasse by asking the front desk and cafeteria to deliver food to my office, where Tru was able to settle into his meal while chatting up his volunteer tutor away from other students.*

*Tru exhibited telltale signs of a prickly personality. In addition, the volunteer tutor and I made assumptions about Tru that impacted our perception of the message he sought to communicate. Throughout this guide, you will learn more about prickly behavior and how your own perceptions can influence porcupine moments.*

You may encounter a prickly porcupine at any time during your youth work career. To cross the communication divide, you need to be familiar with the different behaviors a porcupine might display.

A **porcupine** could be someone who feels threatened or challenged and is

- engaging in angry, regressive conversation;
- experiencing a power imbalance;
- miscommunicating directly or indirectly;
- withdrawing from the discussion; or
- navigating a difficult conversation.

# Engaging in Angry, Regressive Conversation

Porcupines may demonstrate angry, regressive conversation by lashing out at you. These youth might project a hard exterior to protect themselves from the environment. These youth are difficult to get close to or do not let a lot of people into their social circle. Or they might be quick to express physical anger or aggression, quickly changing between moods or becoming defensive and angry in the moment.

It is your job as a youth worker to identify angry or regressive conversation so you can help the youth process their **emotions** and address the underlying need.

Behaviors indicative of an angry or regressive conversation may include the following:

- quickness to express anger
- projection of a defensive or hard exterior
- yelling or shouting above the youth's normal volume
- shifting rapidly between moods
- throwing objects at people or places
- use of negative language or name-calling
- shifting blame
- purposefully doing the opposite of requests
- withdrawing or demonstrating hostile silence
- focusing on anything except the youth worker
- purposefully saying cruel things for a reaction

## KNOW YOUR LIMITS

As a youth worker, you are likely required to complete basic first aid / CPR / AED certification training. In this training, you are taught to assess a scene before approaching, to remain calm, and to know your limits. These same principles apply to interacting with porcupines. Pay close attention to ensure the conversation does not regress to a point that is unsafe for you or the youth for whom you are responsible.

## Field Study: Mariah

*Mariah was a fourteen-year-old student in my class. She dressed well and always had new makeup, manicures, and hairstyles. She was incredibly smart. But she was also quick to anger.*

*Whenever she was confronted with a challenge she didn't know how to handle, Mariah became overwhelmed and left the room. She was also quick to anger when another youth made fun of her appearance or intelligence.*

*I didn't understand why Mariah rapidly shifted from actively engaged to angrily overwhelmed. Her behaviors appeared as though she were lashing out with ill intent, but the patterns told a different story: Mariah was trying to protect her image in front of her peers. When her image was threatened, she raised her quills and angrily removed herself from the situation.*

*My job as a youth worker was to recognize the prickly behaviors and help Mariah address her underlying need—to maintain her image—in a more productive fashion. I observed her behavior through active listening, asking questions, and learning from her why she shut down or left the room. By asking strategic questions, I helped her put her fear into words and identify more useful ways to react when her identity was challenged.*

## Experiencing a Power Imbalance

Porcupines may feel intimidated or threatened by a power imbalance. As a result, they bristle their quills to protect themselves from harm.

Common power imbalances a porcupine may experience relate directly to the characteristics of the porcupine, their peers, or their youth worker. These characteristics include (but are not limited to) age, title, situation, gender identity, religion, culture, societal authority, social economic status, or role within the community.

Being a youth worker places you in a position of authority, which can create a power imbalance between you and the youth you serve. In addition, your specific job type can create an imbalance within the youth work–career hierarchy: A fun soccer coach, for instance, might be more approachable for youth than a school counselor, teacher, or doctor, who hold more formal titles and authority.

Your gender can also influence a porcupine moment. For example, a female-identifying youth might feel very uncomfortable opening up to a male-identifying social worker. Added complexities exist when youth identify as nonbinary, transgender, or other marginalized populations who may feel intimidated, unwelcome, or unable to bring their authentic experience to the table. The resulting gender-influenced power imbalance could trigger reactions that lead to regressive conversation, complete silence, or withdrawal. The imbalance could also trigger miscommunication because the youth does not feel comfortable enough to open up to you as the youth worker.

## Field Studies: Liam and Devyon

*I met eleven-year-old Liam when I worked at a homeless shelter. Several years later, I met Liam in a completely different environment. We both recognized each other immediately, but he lowered his eyes and positioned his body as if he were shrinking from my presence. Why? Because we had a potential power imbalance: I knew a past that he was embarrassed by. I was unable to connect with Liam or his brother during our entire time together because of his concern I might inadvertently reveal their experience with homelessness.*

•••••••

*In one after-school program, I worked with twelve-year-old Devyon. During a one-on-one interaction, I noticed Devyon was posturing, demonstrating his authority, and trying to establish a presence. He puffed up, stood taller, and squared his shoulders. The volume and cadence of his voice increased with intensity.*

*Recognizing the power imbalance was not helping, I took four steps back and confidently sat down at a table. This surprised Devyon. He expected me to react like many youth workers—by posturing and escalating my own intensity. His surprise created an extra pause where I was able to ask him to share his side of the story. Without that pause, our power imbalance would have led to further tension and breakdown in communication.*

Power imbalances can make youth feel marginalized or unheard, impacting their ability to effectively communicate. It is our job as youth workers to recognize potential power imbalances and to continuously seek ways (within our means) to make youth more comfortable despite them. The following behaviors may indicate a power imbalance:

- posturing to demonstrate authority
- pushing the envelope to test authority
- behaving as class clown at inappropriate moments
- exhibiting a submissive demeanor
- offering short, limited responses or remaining silent
- avoiding eye contact
- using body language to shrink away or grow smaller

# Miscommunicating Directly or Indirectly

Porcupine moments arise due to direct and indirect miscommunication.

**Direct miscommunication** occurs when a youth tells you an explicit lie. Usually, this involves ill intent, self-preservation tactics, or a desire to omit damaging information. Consider the following example:

*Jessy comes to you during your after-school program free time to tearfully say Micah hit them for no reason. You take Jessy at their word and punish Micah.*

But what happens if you ask more questions? You might learn Micah was hit first . . . or that Micah hit Jessy because Jessy cheated at the card game they were playing. In this situation, Jessy explicitly lied to you about who started the fight by omitting damaging information.

**Indirect miscommunication** occurs when youth workers miss or misunderstand key aspects of the youth's story. Typically, no ill intent exists when indirect miscommunication occurs; yet the harm or impact can be the same. Indirect miscommunication can also occur when the youth does not have the words to tell their story.

## *Field Study: Zion*

*I worked with Zion, a four-year-old, at a day camp for youngsters. He started to cry during playtime but could not tell me what he needed. Why? Because he didn't have the command of language yet to recognize he was frustrated, hungry, and due for a nap. I was not sure of the root cause of his tears, which caused a brief miscommunication as I sought to narrow down the reasons. While no ill intent existed on my part, the communication breakdown delayed the time to resolution and caused some discomfort to Zion as he continued to cry on the floor in a room full of peers.*

Indirect miscommunication includes white lies—for example, telling a youth five minutes remain until break time when there are actually thirty minutes left. Your intent may be to keep the youth engaged in the activity at hand, but the impact can result in a communication breakdown when the youth later learns you lied.

## *Field Study: Tria*

*In an after-school program I ran, the last fifteen minutes of each session was reserved for free computer time. Some youth, like eight-year-old Tria, were hyper-focused on the computer time. Tria asked me about it every few minutes. I repeatedly promised I'd let her know when it was time. At the final fifteen minutes, I noticed she was very engaged in an activity with another volunteer, so I did not interrupt to let her know it was computer time. Unfortunately, the fifteen minutes flew by, and Tria missed the computer time. She burst into tears, plopped onto the floor, and refused to move.*

*I indirectly miscommunicated by promising to inform Tria when computer time became available and then neglecting to do so. My behavior was misaligned with the information I provided. I ended up letting Tria calm down and play on the computer for fifteen additional minutes as a compromise for my communication error.*

Your job as a youth worker is to recognize when miscommunication occurs and address it promptly. Behaviors associated with direct or indirect miscommunication may include the following:

- not following directions as delivered
- shifting blame to others
- telling explicit lies or half-truths
- exhibiting shifty body language
- remaining silent

## Withdrawing from the Discussion

You might encounter a porcupine who withdraws from the discussion or activity entirely. These porcupines can be difficult to connect with and may stay quiet throughout the entire encounter. Visual examples include a youth who stares at their cell phone during the entire conversation, actively places headphones over their ears after you ask them a direct question or give explicit instruction, or asks to use the restroom every time a specific topic comes up.

### *Field Study: Mingmei*

*Mingmei taught me more than I taught her when I lived in China. When I was her tutor, we met regularly to practice English, talk about her favorite musicians, read Harry Potter, and, of course, laugh. We grew close, but our time together was limited by both my visa and college calendar. On my last day, she refused to see me off. At face value, her actions appeared rude. But her mom explained it best: the thirteen-year-old Mingmei was very sad our relationship was ending and was afraid she would cry too much when she said good-bye. So she withdrew from the conversation and did not see me off.*

Your job as a youth worker is to recognize withdrawal and identify ways to invite porcupines back into the discussion. Common communication-withdrawal behaviors may include the following:

- being quiet and withdrawn
- frequently departing from the room or activity
- being difficult to talk with or get close to
- ignoring or otherwise being unresponsive to directions
- hyper-focusing on a fidget toy, phone, or other gadget instead of the discussion at hand[1]
- exhibiting bad behavior with the intent of being removed from room or activity

## Navigating a Difficult Conversation

Porcupines commonly appear during difficult conversations. These may range in weightiness from learning a new concept to discussions about race, sex or gender, crime, trauma, drugs, religion, politics, family, relationships, mental health, bullying, and beyond. More often than not, the prickly porcupine is unable or unwilling to address the underlying emotions associated with the topic.

Youth are constantly growing, changing, and reorganizing their brain pathways to help process and store information (used for establishing a worldview). This concept is known as *neuroplasticity*. Youth operate in a **learning brain** space until triggered by internal or external stimuli. Triggers can appear logical or illogical and may relate to previous emotional trauma or current inability to process stimuli.

Once triggered, the rational operating center of the brain (neocortex) stops functioning and the emotional mind (amygdala) kicks in to help us act quickly or immediately. This hyper-focused **survival brain** cannot process complex reasoning. It is challenging to reason with porcupines when their brains are in this state.

---

1. Some youth require the use of a fidget to help with focus, social anxiety, or other personal needs. In these cases, additional factors should be considered to determine whether the youth exhibits porcupine behaviors.

# *Field Study: The Miller Brothers*

*The five Miller brothers regularly attended my after-school program. The boys looked forward to playing in the gym, interacting with the "cool" volunteers, and enjoying extended free computer time. It was not uncommon for fights to break out when the boys encountered conflict or other communication differences with peers during open gym or playtime. The older Miller brothers approached conflict with violence, and the younger brothers looked up to them for guidance. When the younger brothers were faced with a challenge, they waited for their older brothers to step in. The behavior the brothers exhibited looked like a survival brain in action with a focus on the fight part of fight-or-flight. This was always a challenge in my after-school program, and I found myself breaking up several fights.*

*One day, the brothers nonchalantly told me about a shooting they'd witnessed while exiting their school bus a few days earlier. This was not the first shooting the Miller boys had witnessed, but it was the first time I'd learned of their experiences.*

*The older brothers had become numb to violence, to the point where they started to see it as a solution to most problems. The younger brothers did not yet have the words to process the experience, so their trauma appeared as more violence: fistfighting, yelling, or pushing other youth. Each brother spoke about the experience differently and was not ready or able to address the underlying emotions they felt related to gun violence in their lives.*

*The additional context helped me to better understand the behavior the Miller brothers exhibited while in my after-school youth program. The information also helped me facilitate a connection to professionals better equipped to help the youth unpack their trauma in a healthy way.*

You might be the youth worker navigating a difficult conversation. However, you might find that the difficult conversation should be referred to a more qualified professional. Know your limits, and recognize how heavier conversations can impact communication and relationships with youth.

## *Field Study: Amaya*

*In another instance, nine-year-old Amaya was working closely with a volunteer in an after-school program. During their time, Amaya showed the volunteer her "sexy pose," described explicit references to sex, and made inappropriate moaning sounds. Amaya's behavior required a difficult conversation. When confronted about her inappropriate behavior, she doubled down on her "sexy pose" and strutted around, telling the adults she wasn't going to listen.*

*Amaya may have seen or experienced some things most nine-year-olds do not know as much about. She also didn't have the words to express her experience in a more productive way. Finally, Amaya felt like we were accusing her of bad behavior, which triggered her brain into survival mode and shut down productive conversation. We recognized our limits and contacted a professional counselor to help Amaya process her experience.*

Another form of difficult conversation is exhibited in learning, which can happen in or outside a classroom. Youth facing a knowledge gap may exhibit porcupine behaviors because they feel challenged and do not know the answer.

Let's apply this to little Timmy learning a new math concept:

*Timmy knows two apples on their desk plus two apples on their neighbor's desk equals four apples. Timmy knows this because they can physically tap each apple while counting, "One, two, three, and four." You ask Timmy to write this as a simple math equation.*

*Timmy writes, "1 + 1 + 1 + 1 = 4." Technically, they are correct. However, you wanted them to write, "2 + 2 = 4," because the two apples are on separate desks.*

*Timmy is not ready to write this equation because the "2 + 2 = 4" concept is still outside their domain of knowledge. After a while, Timmy gives up. Why? Because they were pushed beyond their comfort zone too quickly and with too little support.*

In cases like Timmy's, the risk of pushing through the challenge outweighs immediate needs. When youth are pushed too quickly beyond their comfort level, their brains can become overwhelmed. Overwhelmed brains trigger survival brains, which can cause breakdowns in communication.

## Field Study: River

*Have you ever played "I Win"? The general rules are simple. To win, simply claim, "I win!" and scatter the game pieces, then run away. In the after-school program I ran, this was seven-year-old River's favorite game. We played mancala, checkers, and cards together regularly. Anytime I got close to winning, River would angrily scatter the pieces and walk away.*

*River did not have the words to process or accept losing a game. It was a difficult conversation for her. As a youth worker, I had to help River learn how to process her big emotions when she lost a board game so she could translate these skills to other conversations.*

As a youth worker, you need to be prepared to recognize the underlying emotions that might cause porcupine moments when navigating difficult discussions. Remember, conflict may not always be rational, but it always has a reason. You must help your porcupine navigate these difficult waters. Still, be aware of your own licensure, certification, or professional training limits. There will be times when you need to call in additional support or resources to help resolve a conflict.

Porcupine behaviors in a difficult conversation may include the following:

- crossing arms or legs
- withdrawing from the discussion
- excessively shifting to reposition, fidgeting, or leg bouncing
- frequently changing the subject
- withdrawing, giving up, or otherwise lowering engagement with activity
- clearing the table (e.g., knocks a board game over after losing) or throwing objects
- projecting frustration through tears and/or other nonverbals
- repeating a statement, belief, or seemingly unrelated sentence
- experiencing stomachache or other physical pain
  (stress lives in the mind and body)

In this section, we identified key characteristics of prickly porcupines and when porcupines might appear. The next section explores communication, how it can break
down, and how these breakdowns can lead to porcupine moments. We will spend
more time building up your communication know-how to successfully navigate these
kinds of porcupine moments later in this guide.

## TAKE ACTION: IDENTIFY YOUR PORCUPINES

*Write your answers here or in appendix 1, section 1.*

Describe the porcupines in your life.

When do you typically see porcupines? Consider time of day, location, environment,
activity, and subject matter.

Which prickly porcupine attributes or behaviors do you most frequently encounter?

How do you feel when you encounter a prickly personality?

# Chatter Categories

## Classification: Communication

**Latin:** *communico* (**I share**), *communicare* (**to share**)
**Common:** talk, yak, gab, tweet, slack, chat, listen, write, read, connect

## What Is Communication?

**Communication** is the way in which we send and receive messages. It is how we transmit information to each other through a shared or common system of signs, symbols, or behaviors. We communicate with each other verbally and nonverbally, through visual and auditory channels. Members of the hearing- or sight-impaired communities communicate with each other through a shared or common system of signs, symbols, and behavior but may have slightly modified auditory or visual communication methods when compared to members of the hearing or seeing population.

We spend a significant amount of our waking time connecting with others. We interact in person, over the phone, and via email. We listen to playlists and podcasts;

watch feature films and viral videos; and read books, blogs, and billboards. Each of these interactions involves communication.

It is essential that we as youth workers communicate effectively with youth both to avoid porcupine moments and to de-escalate them when they arise. Authors and communication coaches Gregory Hartley and Maryann Karinch have written extensively on how body language, nonverbals, and human behavior influence communication. They propose that communication can be broken into three categories: verbal, vocal, and nonverbal.

**Verbal communication** recognizes the selection of words we use to convey or share ideas, messages, or needs with others.

## Field Study: Nia

*Nia, a seven-year-old in my summer youth program, was swearing, which was not allowed. I asked Nia to use "different words" to communicate their message. Nia listened—and used different swear words instead. The words I selected to communicate my message were not direct enough to lead to the behavior change I expected (no more swearing). Yet a message and behavior change were communicated. The moral of the story is to ensure the words you select align with the behavior you seek to influence.*

**Vocal communication** recognizes the tone, register, volume, and resonance with which we project our voices as we share ideas, messages, or needs with others. Higher registers coupled with increased pace and volume may project excitement or anxiety. A lower tone and slower vocal pace projects calmness.

Therapists and counselors leverage vocal communication effectively by lowering and slowing their vocal tone and pacing when responding to patients. This helps interrupt stress triggers and recalibrate the limbic system, which plays a pivotal role in behavioral and emotional regulation.

Be mindful of the typical vocal range for the person speaking. Some people naturally project louder or softer than you might expect or be comfortable with. While initially their tone might feel excited, anxious, or angry, they may actually be speaking within their normal vocal range.

RESOURCE

To hear how the human voice can be used as an instrument to project a message, check out Julian Treasure's "How to Speak So That People Want to Listen" TED Talk.

**Nonverbal communication** recognizes the transmission of messages that do not involve words or vocal components. This includes body language, position in the room in relation to an exit or authority figure, gesturing, fidgeting, clothing, posture, and more. In American Sign Language, nonverbal communication includes the pace used to sign a message to convey an emotion, experience, or need. You can pick up on the underlying emotions or messages a porcupine seeks to communicate based on the sum of its nonverbal expressions.

# When Does Communication Break Down?

A **communication breakdown** occurs when the message we try to send is interrupted, incorrectly transmitted, incorrectly received, or misunderstood. Communication breakdowns can occur even if all parties involved experience the same conversation topic, moment, and external cues. Despite shared circumstances, people receive or interpret messages differently based on personal contexts—and these differing interpretations can lead to conflict.

## *Case Study: The Dress Effect*

*The optical illusion took the internet by storm in 2015 when social media users disagreed on the color of a certain dress. Despite looking at the same photograph, viewers perceived the colors differently based on their individual circadian rhythms.*

*The dress is actually black and blue. However, the human brain interprets the wavelengths based on assumptions derived from personal experience with color illumination: People who rise with the sun and go to sleep with the sunset tend to see the dress as white and gold. In comparison, individuals who rise after sunrise and go to sleep after sunset tend to see the dress as black and blue. Researchers coined this experience the "Dress Effect."*

## TAKE ACTION: DRESS EFFECT

*Write your answers here, or turn to appendix 1, section 2.*

Search for the "dress illusion" online. What color(s) do you see?

Optical illusions illustrate how our different backgrounds or experiences can influence our understanding of the same lines, shapes, and spaces. Similarly, a youth might see or hear something in a shared experience or discussion, and the difference can cause miscommunication. Six key categories influence a communication breakdown:

1. Perspectives
2. Perceptions
3. Assumptions
4. Objectives
5. Emotions
6. Styles

# Perspectives

**Perspectives** are the different vantage points from which we approach experiences and communication. Perspectives derive from our varying levels of background information, situational awareness, point of view, and attitude.

Differing perspectives can cause an interruption in the message or incorrect interpretation of the message being sent. As an indirectly involved party, you might be able to better separate yourself from the youth's experience. This separation might make it easier for you to see a different solution, while the youth might be so directly involved they cannot step back and reflect on the bigger picture. Bridging the perspective gap can be challenging.

Youth sometimes expect adults to automatically know all the facts. As a result, they may share the facts *they* believe relevant while omitting information *you* might find relevant. In some cases, youth might omit information for fear of the youth worker's reaction.

As you play catch-up with the youth's story, you are trying to track their own unique perspectives in line with your own perspectives. You might have to ask fact-gathering questions that help you better understand the full picture. This can delay or interrupt your understanding of the message the youth seeks to convey.

## TAKE ACTION: PERSPECTIVES

*Write your answer here or in appendix 1, section 2.*

When have perspectives caused a miscommunication in your work? What was the result?

## Perceptions

**Perceptions** are typically the means through which we understand or interpret a situation through our observations, thoughts, beliefs, attributions, identities, or judgments. Consciously or unconsciously, our thoughts impact the way we communicate. A misplaced perception or unrecognized bias can turn our conversation upside down in an instant.

Ever wonder why it can be so easy to strike up a conversation with someone who shares your favorite sports team? Or grew up in your hometown? Or attended the same summer camp? The answer is **in-group bias:** our automatic tendency (whether consciously or unconsciously) to show preference for people who share certain commonalities with us. Humans developed this ability as an evolutionary survival trait; research suggests it kept early humans safe from disease and conflict with neighboring groups.

Unfortunately, it is typically very difficult for outsiders to join an in-group. In most cases, we consciously or unconsciously extend certain preferences to those who share similar in-group tendencies or characteristics. In some cases, we automatically reject people who do not share our in-group similarities. The way we perceive others or situations can result in these often unintentional communication missteps.

## Field Study: Riley

*I met fifteen-year-old Riley while student teaching a secondary social studies class. Riley projected a hard exterior, rarely raised her hand in class, and disliked being randomly called upon to answer a question. Riley kept to herself and huffed at me a lot during my time as a student teacher. I perceived Riley's behaviors as withdrawn and uninterested in my teaching style. I found myself frequently thinking through ways to try to reengage Riley in classroom learning, with little success. The story I told myself based on my perceptions was that Riley was disengaged and unresponsive to my teaching.*

*At the end of my student teaching experience, I gave all my students a chance to complete a survey where they could offer feedback on my teaching effectiveness. Riley left a lengthy note thanking me for my teaching and lamenting my departure because she believed my teaching style worked better for her learning than the primary classroom instructor's style. She was afraid she would not learn anything from the teacher after I left.*

*Riley's reality was very different from my perception, or the story I told myself based on my observations, thoughts, beliefs, and judgments. I unintentionally miscommunicated with my student because I let my perception get in the way of her lived experience.*

# TAKE ACTION: PERCEPTIONS

*Write your answer here or in appendix 1, section 2.*

It is important to be aware of in-group bias perceptions as a youth worker. What in-group biases might you hold?

How do your in-group biases impact the way you perceive the youth with whom you work?

Could your in-group biases impact the way you communicate with youth? How?

## Assumptions

An **assumption** is something we accept to be true without yet having proof. Part of human communication hinges on making assumptions—doing so helps us jump into conversations and make quicker judgments or decisions throughout the discussion.

However, incorrect assumptions can cause communication breakdowns. Interruptions are a common example. People often interject because they assume the speaker has finished the story. This incorrect assumption may shut down the speaker prematurely, causing the listener to miss out on important details. The phenomenon is well documented in the medical field, which exhibits similarities to (and, in some cases, professional overlap with) youth work.

In the patient-physician relationship, a patient seeks to communicate important information to their physician in hopes of medical attention and guidance in a time of need. As author and physician Dr. Danielle Ofri notes, "The story the patient tells the doctor constitutes the primary data that guides diagnosis, clinical decision-making, and treatment." The physician holds a position of inherent power in which they can deliver potentially life-altering direction based on the information acquired from and assumptions made during the conversation.

Similarly, youth may come to you seeking guidance, support, or direction in their own time of need. The story they tell you constitutes *your* primary data-gathering process—you must listen to the story in full to distinguish what you *hear* from what you are *told* from what you *should* be hearing so you can provide the most appropriate guidance and support.

Both patients and porcupines seek guidance and try to communicate their truths effectively. But what happens when they are interrupted or ignored?

## Case Study: Physician Interruptions

*In the mid-twentieth century, a team of researchers set out to uncover the impact of physician interruptions in the United States. They studied the initial fact-gathering part of the office visit, which is when patients air their concerns and describe symptoms.*

*Researchers found physicians tended to dominate and control 91–99 percent of the conversation through questioning and dialogue. Patients were interrupted an average of 18 seconds after they began sharing their medical concerns. These interruptions led to missed diagnoses, incorrect treatment plans, and misdiagnoses among patients. When left to complete their story uninterrupted, patients spoke for no more than 150 seconds on average, and physicians were able to use the additional information to create more appropriate treatment plans.*

*This early research was conducted at a time when it was the norm for the physician to be the all-seeing knowledge source. It was taboo for patients to ask deeper questions, which could symbolize a challenge to the physician's authority. Follow-up research conducted in 1999 indicated little change despite more progressive social constructs: on average, patients were interrupted or redirected within 23.1 seconds of starting to speak. Patients who were not interrupted or redirected often spoke about 6 seconds longer on average.*

*At the time of this writing, Western cultural norms expect patients to ask their physicians questions and share more of their stories during the initial patient-physician data-gathering interview. It could be hypothesized patients have more latitude to share their full stories with physicians free from interruption. Unfortunately, patients are still interrupted or redirected within an average of 11 seconds—7 seconds quicker than in 1984. Physicians continue to miss key information when they interrupt patients, which leads to misdiagnosis, recurring illness, decline in patient trust, and increase in malpractice lawsuits.*

## Field Study: Abraham

*Early in my career, I worked on a team of youth workers who led after-school activities. Our team also offered preschool-age childcare one night each week so parents could attend a free parenting class.*

*We were excited to welcome a new member to our team, Abraham. He was older than most of us, but because of his prior youth work experience, we assumed he would jump right in and perform well.*

*Unfortunately, Abraham was not willing to assist with the preschool childcare. Instead, he backed all the women into managing these activities. We became frustrated and felt purposefully demeaned. We assumed he was being sexist.*

*Our assumptions eventually led to Abraham's voluntary resignation. Later, we learned that in his community, it is the women's role to take ownership for preschool childcare. Men were not supposed to impose—in fact, he'd assumed his interference would offend the female team members.*

Workplace disputes often occur because one party assumes ill intent. How often have you received an email in all capital letters? To some parties, caps lock signifies yelling. But by assuming aggressive intent, you may inadvertently cause tension or create a communication breakdown—perhaps the sender simply has a broken keyboard.

Always assume best efforts and goodwill on behalf of the other party. This will help frame your response into a more positive, effective reaction.

## TAKE ACTION: ASSUMPTIONS

*Write your answer here or in appendix 1, section 2.*

When have assumptions caused a communication breakdown in your work? What was the result?

How long do you allow youth to speak or share their story before interrupting?

## Objectives

Every communication experience is initiated with at least one **objective**—a goal or a reason. Since communication is a two-way street, it is common for multiple objectives to be present. Think about a social media influencer sharing a short video. Their objective might be to advertise, educate, influence, or share information. Your goal, as the viewer, might be to be influenced or simply to be entertained. Regardless of the creator's objective, your experience is ultimately impacted by whether your own goal was met.

Differing objectives might appear in a youth employment or job coaching program. The youth might come to a meeting ready to ask for a raise, feeling they have done a great job over the last three months of involvement in the program and deserve financial acknowledgment for their best efforts.

You might enter the same conversation with completely different objectives. You may want to discuss the youth's attendance or academic performance. Maybe you have a list of required coaching questions you need to ask. Your objectives might not even allow space for the youth's request.

At the end of the conversation, the youth walks away feeling unheard and defeated. You walk away feeling happy because you checked all the boxes on your meeting agenda. You both experienced a communication breakdown because you did not adequately address the needs of one party. When communicating, consider what *you* want from the conversation compared to what *the youth* might want from the conversation.

## *Field Study: Emily*

*Misaligned objectives caused Emily, my twelve-year-old mentee, to regress in conversation and withdraw from our relationship. I wanted to help her with her schoolwork and offer additional tutoring. Emily wanted to have fun, play games, and explore the community.*

*Because I planned every session around tutoring and academics, Emily started to withdraw and offer one-word answers to my questions. This impacted our relationship until I realized the issue. I made a point to ask Emily what she wanted to do, which helped ensure our meetings met both of our objectives. This simple shift helped create a more enjoyable mentorship experience.*

## TAKE ACTION: OBJECTIVES

*Write your answer here or in appendix 1, section 2.*

In what ways have differing objectives caused communication breakdown in your work?

## Emotions

**Emotions** influence the way we process or receive information, thereby impacting effective communication. Sadness, loss, grief, anxiety, stress, fear; happiness, excitement, contentedness—each of these emotional states impacts the way a message is transmitted for better or for worse.

Anxious, overly energetic, or manic communication styles lead to communication breakdown. Think about

the overly excited youth who spews information at five hundred words per minute. It can be challenging to follow their story at their rapid pace. An energetic youth might also pace, jump, or move around rapidly, which can add (or detract) from the message they seek to communicate.

Hungry, tired, or hangry emotions can cause the brain to process surrounding information too quickly, resulting in errors in judgment or other forms of communication breakdown.

## *Field Study: Grandma's Lesson*

*My grandmother taught me the power of a simple pretzel from an early age. As a teacher, she kept a jar under her desk to help de-escalate hangry porcupines. She always said a student who was truly hungry would accept a pretzel, while a student asking for a snack out of boredom would turn it down as boring, bland, or yucky. She was right. I adopted a similar practice in after-school programs to ensure youth had access to snacks when needed. This practice helped de-escalate several prickly personalities.*

Ultimately, emotions overwhelm the brain and cause communication missteps. This can be especially challenging for youth who cycle through multiple emotions within a few minutes, hours, or day but may not have the communication skills to explain their experience or articulate their needs. In other words, effective communication is not effective until the brain and youth calm down or gain control over their emotions.

# TAKE ACTION: EMOTIONS

*Write your answers here or in appendix 1, section 2.*

What emotions do you see most frequently in youth attending your program?

How do these emotions impact or influence communication in your program?

Consider your own emotions. What raises your quills, aggravates you, or pushes your buttons?

When your quills are up, how does it impact your relationship with youth?

# Styles

Differing communication **styles** inadvertently cause communication breakdown. Style can vary widely between individuals, communities, regions, and cultures. Communication styles also differ across ages. The speaking style of a five-year-old is different from the speaking style of a ten-year-old. As youth learn new ways to communicate their needs, their speaking styles change. Generally, styles fall into five groups: direct, indirect, aggressive, passive-aggressive, and manipulative.

**Direct communicators** focus on the intent of their message by cutting away fluff and delivering succinct statements. Direct communicators "tell it like it is" and may abide by an "honesty is the best policy" approach to conversation. They perceive direct communication to be more respectful because it does not waste the other party's time with side conversations or excuses. For example, a direct communicator may turn down your request with little or no context. To the communicator, the context has little value if the end answer is "No, I'm not interested." This style may feel abrupt to people who prefer softer messages. My favorite direct communicators are toddlers who say things like "You ruined my whole life" or "You look sad."

**Indirect communicators** express themselves with more ambiguity, using nuances, metaphors, or small talk to introduce their intended message. These communications may require the other party to read between the lines. People who prefer indirect communication may perceive the communication style to be more respectful because it provides space for the other party to weigh in, make a decision, feel included, respectfully decline, or otherwise avoid embarrassment. However, this communication style may feel wordy or frustrating to people who prefer direct messages. My favorite indirect communicators are youth who say things like, "I'm not cheating; I'm only helping myself win."

**Aggressive communicators** express their ideas strongly and may demand, command, or leverage sarcasm, often at the expense of others. This communication style focuses on the needs of the speaker and ignores the rights or boundaries of others. Aggressive communicators may tell people, "Get over it," "It's my way or the highway," or "I don't care." Unlike direct communicators, their intent is more about personal needs and less about the needs of the other party involved. This communication style can be frustrating to people when their boundaries are ignored or they are excluded from the discussion.

**Passive-aggressive communicators** share their message with an air of passivity, but the intent comes from a place of aggression or anger. Sarcasm and double entendres are tools passive-aggressive communicators keep in their toolbox. A passive-aggressive communicator might tell you, "Oh, it's okay . . ." followed by a comment designed to demean you or another party (e.g., "Oh, it's okay you sent that email to five hundred plus people . . . it only had two spelling errors."). Passive-aggressive communicators control the conversation with statements designed to *sound* supportive while simultaneously cutting others down.

**Manipulative communicators** leverage a variety of communication tools to express their ideas in a way that bends the other party to their will. Manipulative communicators use crocodile tears, body language, generalized statements, and language designed to make the other party feel sorry for them or guilty enough to take action. Common statements include "Don't you agree?" or "You never have time to help me."

Manipulative communicators may also leverage half-truths, lies, gaslighting, or gossip to encourage the other party to help them. Like aggressive communicators, their intent focuses on personal benefit. I've worked with youth who used manipulative communication styles to guilt staff and volunteer mentors into offering additional snacks or computer playtime (e.g., "I never get to have any fun," "I never get to play on the computer," or "The other cool volunteers let me do this.").

•••••••

Speaking styles may also be heavily influenced by our hometowns. For example, I grew up in Minnesota. In the United States, the Midwest is known for its passive-aggressive, indirect communication style. People on the East Coast, on the other hand, are known to be direct and assertive. When I first encountered people from New York, I interpreted their direct style as aggressive and rude. This interpretation led to some challenging conversations between my East Coast peers and me.

Effective communication begins with the ability to identify porcupines, understand their styles, and approach them with patience, self-awareness, and adaptability. Keep in mind, individual communication styles may shift from person to person and moment to moment. Begin to recognize preferred communication patterns of the youth you serve.

# TAKE ACTION: STYLES

*Write your answer here or in appendix 1, section 2.*

What kinds of communication styles have you encountered in your role as a youth worker?

# Porcupine Plans

## Navigation: ARISE

**Latin:** *surgo* **(I rise, I lift, or I grow)**
**Common:** appear, emerge, stand up, support

So how do we better help our youth embrace their big emotions, navigate the choppy waters of transition, and communicate their unique needs more effectively?

De-escalating and redirecting porcupines starts with you. Think about your communication action plan like a fire drill. We practice safely evacuating a building with regular fire drills to become familiar with what to do in an emergency. We create communication action plans and put them into practice for the same reason. When a porcupine moment arises, it triggers our internal fight-or-flight response. To react calmly and appropriately, we need to be practiced and well versed in communication strategies.

Before trying to de-escalate a porcupine, make sure you know your limits. Consider whether your safety or the safety of others is in immediate jeopardy. Work within your training, licensing, and experience. Recognize sometimes the safest way to de-escalate a porcupine is to remove yourself or others from the space and hand over the situation to someone with more training, expertise, or authority.

# TAKE ACTION: AUDIT AND EXPLORE

*Write your answers here or in appendix 1, section 3.*

## Reflect on Communication Divides

Take a moment to honestly reflect on your communication with prickly personalities. What does it feel like to encounter a prickly personality?

How comfortable are you engaging with a prickly personality?

Describe how you feel when you have successfully redirected or de-escalated a prickly personality.

## Name a Porcupine

The first step in your action plan is to identify a porcupine. Who is the prickly porcupine you want to assist? Where do you encounter this porcupine? How old are they?

This porcupine is _____.

I encounter this porcupine in _____.

This porcupine is about _____ years old.

# ARISE to the Challenge

**ARISE** is a communication tool designed to help you effectively plan for, redirect, and de-escalate porcupine moments:

> **A**ctively listen.
> **R**espond appropriately.
> **I**nclude voices.
> **S**tructure.
> **E**mploy nonverbals.

By using the ARISE methodology, you can create the psychological safety and space porcupines need to feel heard. This tailored approach is especially important given that each porcupine or youth is unique and may require a different response rooted in patience and self-awareness.

## Actively Listen

**Actively listening** shows the porcupine you are approachable and available. The value of listening should not be understated in the field of youth work. Social worker

Catherine de Hueck Doherty once quipped, "With the gift of listening comes the gift of healing." Effective listening can help uncover additional information that may help better serve the youth telling the story.

Traditional conversation and listening theories emphasize "trading monologues." In this scenario, the listener patiently waits with a stoic expression until the speaker stops talking. The trading of monologues does not truly capture active listening or provide full space for the speaker to share their authentic story. For example, imagine sharing an exciting story about how you were given a wonderful birthday present. How would you feel if, as you spoke, the listener stared at you without any expression? Would you believe they were truly interested in what you had to say?

## Case Study: Listeners as Communicators

*A team of Canadian researchers from the University of Victoria studied the role listeners play in communication. Previous research focused on conversations in which the speaker and listener shared a vested interest or were not communicating face-to-face. This new research, however, focused on listeners in face-to-face conversations in which the listener did not have a collaborative role or vested interest in communicating well with the speaker.*

*This first-of-its-kind study uncovered the important role a passive listener plays in communication. The team found a good listener, who exhibits generic and unintrusive conversational cues, serves as a true communication collaborator: speakers used more words and carried the conversation more when listeners reacted with empathy, excitement, or other social cues.*

*The idea that a listener acts as a co-narrator is reinforced by the patient-doctor relationship research we discussed in the Physician Interruptions case study on pages 27—28. Physicians with strong communication backgrounds used minimal sounds, small encourages[2], and other signs of engagement while listening. By allowing patients to share without interruption, these physicians were more likely to accurately solicit patient concerns.*

---

2. *Encourages* are communication nudges designed to keep a conversation going without interrupting the speaker. Published research in this space refers to these communication nudges (or encouragements) as encourages.

CEO Richard Branson works with businesspeople to improve their networking skills. His number one recommendation is to listen more than you talk. Research in the field of social psychology finds the person who does the most *talking* in a conversation feels a *deeper connection* to the other party. Conversely, the person who spends more time *listening* feels *less connected*.

As a youth worker, it is not your job to feel a deep connection to prickly youth. Rather, it is your job to create the psychological safety and space for the *porcupine* to feel connected to *you*. Active listening creates this space by giving the porcupine room to freely express their story.

The hardest part of active listening is to avoid thinking about your next response. The human brain can process about 800 spoken words per minute, but the average native English speaker delivers about 125 words per minute. This leaves a lot of space for our minds to wander while waiting for someone to complete their thoughts. Try to suppress any immediate thoughts or statements as they cross your mind—these interruptions distract you from the porcupine's emotional, physical, or social needs. Stay present and in the moment throughout the story. One way to practice relaxing your mind is through meditation. I recommend you practice this on your own and *not* during a porcupine moment.

# TAKE ACTION: ACTIVELY LISTEN

*Write your answer here or in appendix 1, section 3.*

Practice staying present with meditation.

1. Find a relaxing position seated or lying down in a quiet space.
2. Start to focus on your breath, breathing in for a count of four and out for a count of four. Pause between breaths.
3. Notice tension drip away from your jaw. Let your neck and shoulders relax.
4. Allow your elbows to release and fingers to fall away from your body.
5. Notice any tension in your hips—let it go.
6. Allow your knees and ankles to release.
7. Try to clear your mind of any thoughts. If a thought enters, notice it, acknowledge it, and let it go. Stay here for as long as is comfortable, letting your thoughts fall away.

Reflect on your meditative experience here.

As a youth worker, you have an incredible ability to change the lives of the youth you serve. Consider the impactful youth workers in your own life. What characteristics did they bear? Often, the mentors who stand out to us as we get older are the ones who took the time to listen. As you continue your meditation journey, you will become better adept at actively listening to porcupines, focusing on their needs, and responding appropriately.

# TAKE ACTION: ACTIVELY LISTEN

*Write your answers here or in appendix 1, section 3.*

Write down three ways to practice active listening today.

1.

2.

3.

## Respond Appropriately

When communicating with youth, ensure your response is age appropriate as well as developmentally and situationally appropriate. The way you respond to a five-year-old should be different from how you respond to a ten-year-old or a teenager—and that is okay. Reactions should be developmentally appropriate for the age group or developmental stage to which the porcupine belongs.

There are three key ways to frame an appropriate response to prickly porcupines:

1. Accessing assertive responses.
2. Articulating needs through questioning.
3. Activating minimal encourages.

### *Accessing Assertive Responses*

Assertive responses communicate one idea at a time to help your porcupine process their experience. These are single statements that get to the root cause or issue impacting the porcupine. Assertive responses can also be used to help porcupines plan and problem-solve.

Think about how you craft responses to porcupines. Do you trail off in a sentence? Throw multiple comments into one sentence? Express your own emotions? Ask a series of quick questions? These rapid-fire thoughts can overwhelm a porcupine in the moment. Consider responding with single-idea or single-sentence comments to help the porcupine process one item at a time.

•••••••

A certain level of **emotional intelligence** can help you level up your assertive response. Emotional intelligence is the act of perceiving emotions, understanding emotions, regulating emotions in oneself or others, and using emotions to facilitate cognitive activities. As a youth worker, you may already have a high level of emotional intelligence, which helps you tap into the needs and experiences of the youth you serve.

Author and mediator Douglas E. Noll, JD, MA, recommends the use of **affect labeling** to identify and name big emotions. This is the practice of labeling the primary emotion you hear coming through. Start by ignoring all the *words* your porcupine is using and instead focus in on the *emotion* you hear in their voice and see in their physical posture.

Use that information to name the emotion you think the porcupine is projecting. You could use a phrase such as, "I can see you are angry." Practice verbalizing the emotion until the porcupine agrees with you. If the porcupine repeats a statement or phrase, try saying a different emotion. Keep naming emotions until the porcupine calms down or agrees with your label.

## Field Study: Landon

*I spent many years as a lifeguard in my community, which meant I spent some time jumping into the water to retrieve drowning or distressed kiddos from the pool. I became used to the youth being frightened, embarrassed, and anxious after their traumatic experience. Landon was one of these kiddos. After I pulled him from the water, he began crying uncontrollably. I used affect labeling to interrupt the survival brain and helped him process the experience by saying, "You are scared. It's okay to be scared and sad. This was a scary experience for you." I repeated the statements until Landon calmed down and was ready to talk about what happened.*

Affect labeling is especially pertinent when working with youth still developing their prefrontal cortexes through their early twenties. Research demonstrates that the act of labeling emotions interrupts the activity occurring in the amygdala, giving space for the porcupine to pause, reassess, and transition into a calmer state.

## Articulating Needs through Questioning

Take your active listening one step further by responding with positive, inclusive language that paraphrases or clarifies key points. Use **targeted questioning** to move the conversation forward through a combination of open- and close-ended questions. This will help you better interpret the story the porcupine is *telling* versus the story you are *hearing*—and the story you *should* be hearing—so you can determine next steps together.

**Open-ended questions** are used to make people feel important or understand a point of view. They also help get porcupines talking. In the medical research we discussed in the Physician Interruptions case study, physicians who used open-ended questions learned more about the patients' underlying needs than physicians who used close-ended questions.

Similarly, you can use open-ended questions to give the porcupine space to share their story and demonstrate you are truly listening, hearing, and reacting to their concerns. Examples of open-ended questions include the following:

- What brings you here today?
- What can I do for you today?
- Can you tell me more about . . . ?
- What's the best ___ for . . . ?
- Can you tell me the story of . . . ?
- What are the consequences if . . . ?
- Have you experienced this . . . ?
- What do you think about . . . ?
- How do you . . . ?

**Strategic questions** are open-ended and are asked with a targeted purpose. They are often used to maximize the likelihood of getting the porcupine to say yes but by placing the power in their hands. Examples of strategic questions include the following:

- If I send you this, could you look at it before we meet next?
- Would it be okay for me to call your parent/guardian for you?
- What if we did . . . ?
- Would it be okay for me to talk with _____ about what we just discussed?
- Can you tell me what you're thinking about now that we've talked?
- What did I miss?
- What questions do you have?
- Would it be okay for me to offer some advice? Or do you just need me to listen?

Open-ended questions can help you explore the underlying root cause of a prickly porcupine moment. As you learn more about the porcupine's needs, start using strategic questions to guide the conversation toward potential resolution.

## Case Study: Targeted Questioning

*One teacher I worked with used targeted questioning to manage a student who didn't want to finish their work and was starting to become a distraction in the class. In other words, the student was becoming a porcupine. The teacher worked with the student to uncover an action plan and gain alignment on next steps:*

**Teacher:** *Can you tell me what's on your mind?*
   **(open-ended)**

**Student:** *I don't want to redo this bull crap.*

**Teacher:** *How many missing assignments do you have left to do?*
   **(open-ended)**

**Student:** *Two.*

**Teacher:** *Oh, that's not too bad.*

**Student:** *I don't want to do it.*

**Teacher:** *How many times do you want to retake this class?*
    **(strategic)***I know you can do this.*
**Student:** *Fine. I'll do it in a minute.*
**Teacher:** *Can I check back with you in a few minutes?* **(close-ended)**
**Student:** *Sure.*

**Close-ended questions** are typically used to close a deal or agree on next steps. These questions usually elicit a dichotomic response in which there are only two options: yes or no. Some examples include the following:

- Do you agree?
- Can we do this/that?
- Do you have questions?
- Are you ready?
- Are you hungry?
- Are you listening?

# Field Study: Kayden

*Kayden was an eight-year-old in my summer activity program. Halfway through our walk to the park, he plopped down in the middle of the sidewalk. Kayden refused to stand up or move, having become bored and tired in the midafternoon sun. As a youth worker, I could negotiate with Kayden, threaten Kayden with lost privileges or a write-up, or seek to identify the root cause and come up with a creative way to address Kayden's need. I noticed Kayden was tired and frustrated with our pace. I needed Kayden to keep going because the alternative was turning back, which could create a prickle among the other youth on the walk.*

*I paused and considered my options before asking Kayden a simple close-ended question: "Do you want a piggyback ride?" Kayden's face lit up, and the prickly porcupine moment was paused. A piggyback ride was the creative solution I could offer Kayden at that moment in time. For some youth workers, piggyback rides are not a viable option. Creatively think through the options available to you and use questions to navigate toward a solution.*

Effective questions should be paired with purposeful **wait time.** This principle is used frequently in classrooms, live presentations, and training events. After asking a question, pause and wait. Give the porcupine space to process your question or comment before adding more commentary. Remember, their brain chemistry is likely under the influence of "survival brain," in which it can process only one thing at a time. So give the porcupine extra space to think quietly.

If you're uncomfortable with silence, count to ten in your head while waiting.

## TAKE ACTION: TARGETED QUESTIONS

*Write your answers here or in appendix 1, section 3.*

Write down three open-ended questions you already use.

1.

2.

3.

Write down three open-ended questions you want to start using.

    1.

    2.

    3.

Write down three close-ended questions you already use.

    1.

    2.

    3.

Write down three close-ended questions you want to start using.

    1.

    2.

    3.

## Activating Minimal Encourages

Strategically placed **minimal encourages** empower the speaker to carry on with their story. You can nod, smile, or express excitement or anticipation at appropriate moments. You can also use short phrases or noises to nudge the storyteller to continue speaking. These small verbal or nonverbal responses add commentary to demonstrate that you are tracking the speaker's experience or story and encourage them to continue.

While comments like "Uh-huh," "I'm following," and "Tell me more" may interrupt the flow of the story, they do not stop the discussion (Marvel et al., 1999, 283–87). Strategic use of encourages helps empower the communicator to pursue the flow of the story, much like gravity helps propel water along the current in a river.

Minimal encourages may include nonverbal cues as well as the following comments:

- "Yes . . ."
- "Uh-huh . . ."
- "Okay . . ."
- "I see . . ."

## TAKE ACTION: MINIMAL ENCOURAGES

*Write your answer here or in appendix 1, section 3.*

Write down three minimal encourages you can start using today.

1.

2.

3.

# Include Voices

Youth act in ways that address their unmet needs. Such actions might be perceived as porcupine behavior when it should be perceived as an act of self-preservation. The Fundamental Interpersonal Relationship Orientation model, developed by Dr. Will Schutz, suggests we can avoid conflict by satisfying three key needs: inclusion, control, and affection.

The need for inclusion is a key element we must recognize for our youth—they seek to be seen and heard. People want a seat at the table and to be included in the conversation. There are three ways you can help meet the need for inclusion:

1. Engage youth.
2. Recognize your limits.
3. Leverage inclusive language.

## *Engage Youth*

Youth voices are often excluded by the inherent nature of youth programming design. Programs are developed and implemented based on adult-identified objectives: adults hold the positions of authority; adults create the rules; and adults establish the missions and initiatives based on their own objectives and assumptions.

Youth input is often unsolicited or excluded in this approach. This results in a power imbalance in which the youth worker ignores or is unaware of the needs of the youth, causing porcupine moments or communication breakdowns.

## *Field Study: Open Gym*

*During college, I developed and implemented fitness games for after-school program participants, using existing programming and activities. I noticed most of the gym participants skewed male. Female participants tried to participate but became disengaged quickly.*

*I tried all sorts of fancy program and classroom management tactics to keep more female participants engaged longer. No success. Finally, I asked a few of the female students why they no longer participated. I quickly learned they did not like the games the boys always picked. The female participants wanted a variety of games in which their own unique skill sets could add value. By simply asking, I was able to help redesign an after-school gym activity so more youth participated and felt engaged.*

Input panels or committees are one way to enhance the program experience directly through youth voices. These groups grant youth their own leadership opportunities as well as a space to provide feedback to adult program leaders.

An example is the Minnesota-based PACER Center's Youth Advisory Board. Members of the Youth Advisory Board are teens served by the organization who participate in regular meetings, present at conferences or staff training, provide input on publications, and communicate with elected officials on organization initiatives. The Youth Advisory Board helps provide insight and guidance to PACER leadership to drive effective and useful programming for its members. I saw members of the Youth Advisory Board present their work when I attended the annual PACER Symposium. I was blown away by the amount of insight and value they brought to the event as they shared their personal experiences living with exceptionalities or disabilities and how PACER helped them learn skills, succeed in school, or access the support they needed in their communities.

Another example is the Minnesota Youth Council (MYC), which seeks to engage middle and high school students across Minnesota in outreach, education, and advocacy efforts at the state capitol. The MYC is written into Minnesota statute, under the 2013 Minnesota Youth Council Bill, to serve as the official voice of youth to the state legislature and governor's office. The MYC is recognized as a special committee with the ability to introduce legislation around health and wellness, environmental justice, education equity, and juvenile justice. It was the first of its kind to be established by law in Minnesota and is a great way to ensure youth voices have a place of influence in the state legislature. Today, youth advocates and members of the MYC work together with adult mentors and legislators to conduct surveys on issues young Minnesotans care about, lead educational summits, coordinate youth advocacy days at the capitol, and issue statements on existing policies. They've even developed documentaries on the impact of substance abuse in young people to help communicate with policy-makers.

It is important to notice whose voices are not being heard and to then take action to include them. Ask strategic questions to identify the unheard voices in your program. Evaluate the impact of their omission. Then set aside your ego and relinquish some authority. Gather, review, and implement youth recommendations. Explore ways to better include them in program activities, design, rule-making, and other engagement. Doing so will empower them to proactively drive change in their communities—ultimately serving not only as a de-escalation tactic but as a proactive way to avoid future conflict.

# TAKE ACTION: INCLUDE VOICES

*Write your answers here or in appendix 1, section 3.*

In what ways does your organization bring to the table the voice of the youth you serve?

What questions or tactics can you use to **include** others in the conversation? Write them down.

1.

2.

3.

4.

5.

6.

## *Recognize Your Limits*

Sometimes you are not the right person to be engaging with or attempting to de-escalate the porcupine. Recognizing you have done all you can or when another youth worker might be able to do a better job is an integral part of communicating with porcupines. To include voices in this way, it might be as simple as bringing in a third party with whom the porcupine has a stronger relationship to assist with the conversation.

## *Field Study: Donte*

> *I worked with Donte in an after-school program. For whatever reason, Donte did not listen to my authority and frequently disregarded program rules. However, Donte had a great relationship with a volunteer he respected and listened to. I recognized my limits but leveraged the youth's perceived authority of the volunteer to reinforce expectations and redirect Donte when his behavior became inappropriate or distracting. The volunteer was able to redirect and de-escalate Donte's behavior by reinforcing my expectations in a way Donte respected. It is okay to recognize individual limits and leverage other resources when necessary.*

As part of your appropriate and inclusive response, you may need to relinquish some conversational authority. This means setting aside your own ego and emotional needs in the moment. Resist the urge to maintain power. This is hard! Our automatic response when someone challenges our authority is to double down and become defensive. Resist your own anger when your power or control is challenged. Give up some of the conversational authority by removing your ego from the experience. Focus on what the porcupine communicates to you, and set aside your own emotional needs when possible.

Sometimes you have to say no. In these situations, seek to honor the porcupine's truths while still presenting facts, data, or rules when appropriate. This might come into play with older youth when we are required to report certain incidents as part of our role as mandated reporters. Youth may come to you and specifically ask you to keep their concerns private. Yet you are unable to do so because of mandated reporting laws. In these situations, it might be best to be honest with the youth and tell them you have to report certain things. I met one youth worker who made it clear at the outset of a difficult conversation with a youth that he was a mandated reporter. Then he gave the youth power in the moment by asking if the youth wanted to help him make the report. In this instance, the youth felt empowered to place the report with the assistance of the youth worker.

Each situation, conversation, and porcupine moment is unique. Make sure you recognize your limits to avoid overpromising or saying things you cannot see through. And when possible, help the porcupine articulate their needs and take action.

## *Leverage Inclusive Language*

Consider how your language includes or excludes voices. Do you use gender-neutral language when addressing groups of people? Do you put the person before the descriptor when explaining your friend lives with a mental or physical health disability?

Giving thought to the language you use can help de-escalate prickly personalities. It can also help prevent prickly situations from arising in the first place. Developing and implementing inclusive language takes focus and is a lifelong journey as cultures, languages, and individuals evolve. Start by examining your own language and replacing words, phrases, or terms that no longer serve you. Then, over time, regularly revisit and update your word choices. These are a few of my favorite inclusive alternatives:

| Exclusive Term | Inclusive Alternative |
|---|---|
| bossy | leader, organizer |
| disabled person | person who lives with a disability or exceptionality |
| ghetto | neighborhood, enclave, home, locality, place |
| guys/gals | folks, folx, y'all |
| handicap | disability, exceptionality |
| lame | boring, lackluster, unimpressive |
| man (e.g., manpower) | human, people |
| underrepresented | marginalized, excluded, disenfranchised |

"Yes, and . . ." is a popular improv activity used to demonstrate the impact that inclusive and exclusive language can have on conversation. **Yes, and statements** use inclusive language to build on the experience and truth of the speaker. *Yes* validates the speaker while *and* helps structure the next layer of experience or discussion. A *yes, and* attitude can help you build on the porcupine's emotion while moving the conversation toward resolution. Consider using *yes, and* statements like the following:

- Yes, you are mad . . . and I am here to help.
- Yes . . .and the assignment is due tomorrow. What do you need from me?
- Yes, you are sad . . . and I am here to listen.
- Yes, you did your best . . . and I am proud of you.
- Yes . . . and we can talk about this. Would you like to talk now?
- Yes . . . and I can listen. What would you like to share?
- Yes . . . and we can tackle this together.

## TAKE ACTION: INCLUSIVE ALTERNATIVES

*Write your answers here or in appendix 1, section 3.*

### Leverage Inclusive Language and Replace Exclusive Language

Which words would you add to the table on page 56?

### Yes, and . . .

Complete the "Yes, and . . ." activity in appendix 2. Which round did you prefer?

# Structure

As discussed earlier, porcupines operate in an overstimulated survival brain mode. You need to help them lay out clear, rational next steps. But to reach those steps, you must help the porcupine transition into a new level of communication, learning, or understanding. This can be achieved by structuring the conversation.

In education, **instructional structuring,** or **scaffolding,** occurs when an educator builds on a student's experiences and knowledge to enhance their learning and aid in the mastery of tasks. Psychologist Lev Vygotsky first introduced this approach with his Zone of Proximal Development theory.

Vygotsky argued learners exist in the zone of achievement, which is represented by what learners or youth can do *now,* in the present. Learners can do some things with the structured support of an educator, mentor, or more advanced peer. With this support, the learner can transition into a new level of learning or understanding.

Similarly, a porcupine needs your support to build their own communication skills so they can better manage their big emotions. The actual conflict resolution itself is less important than the support you provide during the process. Consider the following example:

> *You notice Nyla is breathing heavily and becoming tense when showing you how they play with building blocks. From your perspective, Nyla looks very stressed and concerned about the interaction. You can help them process their emotions by verbalizing the behavior and asking how they feel: "Nyla, I notice you are breathing heavily. How do you feel right now?"*
>
> *Such a simple question can help Nyla dial into their emotions and begin to put words to the experience. This is just one way you can support a porcupine through structured conversation.*

In every porcupine moment, you must acknowledge the emotion to validate the experience through **empathy-based listening** before you can discuss a solution, explore resolutions, and agree on a proposed action. Transitioning through a structured conversation toward resolution helps porcupines grow and build out their own conflict resolution tool kit. To achieve this, you need to give porcupines a sense of purpose and empowerment before asserting a direction, order, or conclusion. In other words, you need to bring them along for the journey. You can do this by following five clear steps:

1. Introduce what you plan to discuss before jumping in.
2. Explain the reason for what you are saying as you say it.
3. Be clear and concise.
4. Empathize.
5. Agree and take action.

## Field Study: Pria

*Look at how a structured conversation helped seven-year-old Pria feel better about reading during quiet time in an early-childhood program. I used the statements below to help Pria warm up to reading time after she had given up, thrown her book aside, and begun pouting.*

| | |
|---|---|
| *Introduce* | *I am sorry you feel alone and unsupported in this experience.* |
| *Explain* | *It is reading time, so we need to focus on this book.* |
| *Be clear* | *I can help.* |
| *Empathize* | *I know it can be frustrating to read a book with so many unfamiliar words.* |
| *Agree and take action* | *I am going to read the words aloud. Can you follow the words on the page with your finger while I read?* |

## *Introduce*

**Introduce what you plan to discuss before jumping in.** You can describe the purpose, preview the next steps, and prepare your porcupine for the next transition. For example, compare these two statements:

1. We are here to discuss your math assignment. We will spend the next thirty minutes reviewing your work so you are ready for tomorrow's test.
2. You need to do your math homework.

The first statement helps the porcupine prepare for the thirty-minute time commitment, the homework review, and the test preparation. The second statement asserts a broad need, which can leave the youth with questions surrounding the activity's purpose, length, and reason.

Another way to introduce next steps is to *preview* and *prepare*. Educators and after-school program activity coordinators do this well when they call out, "Five minutes before our next activity!" Telling youth a transition is about to occur gives them space to wind down their current activity and prepare for the next steps.

## *Explain*

**Explain the reason for what you are saying as you say it.** For example, "We wash our hands to prevent the spread of germs" explains the purpose of a rule while also noting a desired activity change. This sets the stage for the next part of the conversation.

## Field Study: You Could Get Hurt!

*An example I like to use comes from my days as a lifeguard and pool program activity coordinator at a community-based youth center. We served youth ages five to seventeen who lived in the surrounding neighborhood. These youth frequently ran on the pool deck with flagrant disregard for the posted No Running signs. Shouting ("Stop running!") had very little effect. Yet changing my direction to include variations with explanations about why the rule mattered helped decrease the instances of on-deck running—for example, "Stop running, because you could get hurt."*

## Be Clear

Get straight to the point (pun intended). Omit erroneous words or phrases from your instruction, and give directions in *single-concept statements*. Youth sometimes have trouble with phrases containing too much information. Think about the "Keep It Simple" principle or the "rule of threes." Try to break down complex directions into simple concepts the porcupine's brain can easily latch onto. Yes, you might have to repeat your clear, concise direction a few times before it sinks in. That's okay.

This is especially important when we are stressed or in conflict. The rational operating center of the brain (neocortex) stops functioning, and the emotional mind (amygdala) kicks in to help us act quickly or immediately. The emotional mind is responsible for our fight-or-flight mindsets but can only process short, simple pieces of information at a time. Maintaining clear, concise statements that get directly to the intended point help ensure the porcupine has a better chance of understanding the direction.

## TAKE ACTION: CLEARLY EXPLAIN

*Write your answer here or in appendix 1, section 3.*

How might you restate a rule to easily explain its importance in your program? Write out a restatement now:

## Empathize

Validate the porcupine's emotion through empathy-based listening. In this practice, your primary objective is to identify what the porcupine is experiencing. Show them you seek to understand their perspective by actively listening and picking up on the bread crumbs they leave for you during your encounter:

- Here's the deal . . .
- I don't think you understand . . .
- You just don't get me . . .

These statements allow you to ask empathy-based questions in return:

- What would be helpful right now?
- How can I best support you right now?
- Would it be helpful to hear what helped me in a similar situation?
- Do you want to tell me how you are feeling?

Demonstrating empathy is a great way to establish rapport and reassure the porcupine you can be a trusted resource. By demonstrating you care, you create space where the porcupine feels safe to move through the conflict-resolution process.

Hostage negotiator Scott Tillema explains in his 2016 TED Talk how to have a productive conversation with people in crisis through empathy-based listening. He posits the way to effectively communicate in a crisis or conflict is to first seek to understand. Then summarize the person's experience with all the words they used—and with all the emotion they used to deliver those words—to get the person to a point of saying, "Yes, that's right." It is at this point of understanding and acknowledging that the conversation can move into the next Zone of Proximal Development, where decisions can be made together. Demonstrate your level of care through empathy-based listening to help de-escalate prickly situations.

## Field Study: Aliyah

*I met Aliyah when I worked at a summer program for children of mothers living at the housing center. Aliyah was a shy youth who attended the program.*

*She did not like to play much with other kids and especially resisted lying down for nap time. One day, I asked Aliyah to tell me more about why she didn't like nap time. I expected the usual responses from youth her age—"I'm not tired" or "I'm too big for a nap."*

*Instead, Aliyah fidgeted with her hair and said, "You wouldn't understand." Intrigued, I asked her to help me understand. Aliyah fidgeted some more, tried to change the subject, and told me it didn't matter.*

*I noticed concern in her voice and her focus on playing with her long hair. So I pivoted slightly: "You have really pretty hair. Do you do anything fun with it?"*

*This slight change of subject helped Aliyah become more comfortable with me. After some back and forth, she finally revealed she had recently caught head lice. She was nervous that if she caught it again from getting too close to other kids or lying down on a program cot, her mom would be disappointed in her. She told me I couldn't understand "because adults don't get head lice."*

*I replied, "Wow, having head lice must have been really hard for you and your mom." Aliyah agreed. I asked, "Now that I know this, what would make you more comfortable during nap time?" Together, we worked out a plan for her to quietly read in a nearby chair during nap time instead of lying down. Empathetic listening helped create a more welcoming environment for Aliyah to safely relax.*

## TAKE ACTION: DEMONSTRATE EMPATHY

*Write your answer here or in appendix 1, section 3.*

Write three empathy-based questions you can use to establish rapport with youth in your program.

1.

2.

3.

## Agree and Take Action

The end goal for most prickly situations is to reach agreement and take action. To move through the Zone of Proximal Development, the porcupine must be able to articulate their needs: "Yes, I am angry," or "Yes, I am sad," or "Yes, I am tired and frustrated."

Once the porcupine agrees with your affect label, you must offer a tangible action plan to move toward healing. This could be as simple as agreeing to apologize to the bully they punched or agreeing to bring their concerns to another trusted youth worker before allowing the situation to escalate again. In some instances, this may simply be acknowledging they are not okay today but might be better tomorrow. Help the youth take action to move forward, experience conflict resolution, and transition away from the porcupine experience.

## Bounce-Back Statements

I like the use of **bounce-back statements** to structure conversations toward resolution. Bounce-back statements describe expected behavior in a positive light. They are designed to empower, rather than put down, by phrasing instructions in ways that make it okay to try again. For example, rather than saying, "You stopped writing," you might say, "Pick up your pencil and continue writing like I know you can."

# Field Study: Young Allegra

*One experience I had as a young kindergartner has stayed with me through adulthood. My classmates and I were sitting in a circle on the floor while our teacher read to us. I was tired, probably because we had just eaten a snack and had been sitting for a long time.*

*At some point during the story, I yawned. My teacher stopped reading aloud, locked eyes with me, and said, "That was rude. Do not do that again."*

*I was shocked. After all, I was sitting crisscross-applesauce on the floor, with my body facing the teacher. Yes, I had yawned. But how was that wrong?*

*What I did not understand at that time was people could yawn quietly. As a kindergartner, I saw all my cartoon friends yawning loudly on TV. I mimicked the sound in my own yawns because I thought it was expected behavior. In class, the loud noise had inadvertently interrupted my teacher and classmates.*

*If my teacher had used a bounce-back statement like, "Please yawn quietly next time," I would have better understood my error. I might have still felt embarrassed for being called out, but at least I would have been able to recognize how to improve.*

When a porcupine starts to exhibit stressed behaviors, you can use bounce-back statements paired with a question to help them pause, reflect, and put words to their experience. For instance, you might say, "I notice you are breathing heavily. Can you tell me how you are feeling?" The porcupine might not be aware of their heavy breathing. Your bounce-back statement observes the behavior but couples it with a question to gently guide the youth toward the desired behavior—lower stress level or better self-regulation.

## Field Study: Fitness Class

*As a group fitness instructor, I regularly use bounce-back statements to help my class participants exhibit better posture or body mechanics. I will say, "Tuck your hips and pull your belly toward your spine," instead of, "Don't stand with poor posture."*

*The first statement is a clear, concise direction that helps the class participant explore how to position their own body to stand with better posture. The second statement means nothing to someone who does not know how to stand with good posture. If the class participant felt as though they already had good posture, now I've demeaned them as a person.*

*Flipping the statement to omit negatives while including explicit instructions helps empower my class participants to find the proper posture and alignment necessary to continue exercising without risk of injury. In this way, I use bounce-back statements to structure my direction for effective communication.*

# TAKE ACTION:
# BOUNCE-BACK STATEMENTS

*Write your answers here or in appendix 1, section 3.*

Rewrite the statements below as bounce-back statements:

1. You stopped writing.

2. You made a mess.

3. Stop running around the pool.

4. Stop picking your nose.

5. You didn't wash your hands before eating.

Now write your own bounce-back statements. Consider statements you can use with your youth today.

1.

2.

3.

## Employ Nonverbals

Nonverbal communication is essential to our daily exchange of information with those around us. Nonverbal communication includes everything that is happening outside of the words used and all human voice components that do not include the words used. This includes body language, position in the room in relation to an exit or authority figure, fidgeting, clothing, posture, and more. Nonverbal communication might take the form of sitting in silence together to give the porcupine plenty of wait time and silence to process their thoughts. Silence is good. It means the porcupine is still engaged with you. Porcupines who completely shut down might try to leave the situation, but porcupines who stay near you while remaining silent are still engaged—even if they appear to have their nose buried in an electronic device. You can pick up on the underlying emotions or messages a porcupine seeks to communicate based on nonverbal expressions.

## *Field Study: Leah*

*Preteen Leah appeared uninterested in participating in the planned activities. She slouched in her chair, refused to engage with others, and did not put her phone down once. Every nonverbal message she sent appeared to communicate she did not want to be part of the program.*

*When I approached Leah to check in, she kept her nose buried in her phone. However, I noticed she'd stopped typing. Leah was listening, despite the primary nonverbal cues. This was my in. I was heartened by her slight shift in behavior and adjusted my approach accordingly.*

*Instead of telling Leah she needed to put the phone away, I gave her transition time to finish her phone activities and join the group in five minutes. I used a strong posture, confident voice, and unwavering expectation that she follow through. I then walked away to give Leah space to process. She joined her peers in fewer than five minutes after our talk.*

## *Physical Body Positioning*

Recognizing a porcupine's nonverbal signals is only half the equation. You also need to consider your own nonverbals. Notice your proximity to the porcupine. For educators, an easy classroom-management technique is to physically move in front of or near the porcupine while delivering a lecture or instructions. Your physical presence helps communicate that they need to stop the offending behavior or at least pay more attention in the moment.

Consider the level a porcupine operates on, and make sure you are on their same level during the discussion. When I worked with kindergartners, I made a point to kneel so I could hear their concern and look them in the eye. If you are a tall adult and the porcupine uses assisted mobility technology, like a wheelchair, make sure you lower yourself down to their level. Bend over, sit in a chair, or make your way down to the floor. Simply changing your position can help de-escalate the situation by demonstrating empathy or interest.

●●●●●●●

It is very important for youth workers to exhibit positive, nonthreatening body language. This can include setting aside all distractions, physically turning in the direction of the porcupine, or tracking the speaker with your eyes and ears.

Remain self-aware: Are you holding something in a potentially threatening manner? Are your hands above your shoulders or calmly resting by your waist? If sitting behind a desk, are your hands resting on the tabletop or hidden in your lap? Use positive body positioning to establish a safe and supportive environment in which your porcupine can let down their quills. Notice your placement in the physical space. Standing too far away may project disinterest; however, standing too close may increase tension. Are you blocking the exit? For some prickly porcupines, this may signal entrapment and heighten anxiety. This can also put you in danger because the porcupine might feel the need to physically get past you to get to the door.

## Physical Expressions

Have you ever had to give a presentation or pitch something to a group of friends? How did it feel when the audience sat up tall and looked at you as you spoke? It probably felt pretty good. Your audience conveyed interest to you, which helped empower you to continue your pitch.

Porcupines feel similar support when you sit or stand tall to demonstrate engagement. Crossed arms, wandering eye contact, distractedness with devices, or slouching posture can convey disinterest and cause the porcupine to withdraw without resolution.

Your facial expressions can also shut a conversation down. Porcupines come to you in a moment of vulnerability. A judgmental look, even by accident, can add salt to the wound and further escalate the situation. Check your facial expressions and try to maintain a neutral disposition.

•••••••

The body's first physical response to tense situations is to take shorter breaths—or forget to breathe altogether. Short, tense breathing changes your physical body posture and vocal tone. You can help de-escalate a porcupine by simply regulating your own breath.

I attended a conference during which one panelist explained how she used the power of yoga breathing to de-escalate tense boardroom moments. Whenever she noticed the tension rising, she would take a slow, deep breath . . . and immediately feel its impact. Deep breathing brought her shoulders out of her ears, dropped her voice to a lower register, and helped her command the room. The other boardroom attendees would subconsciously notice her new posture and vocal register and begin mirroring the calmer presence.

## Field Study: Ms. Birdseye

*During a particularly intense class session, one of my students said, "Ms. Birdseye, you gotta take a breath." They were right—the rowdy class energy had elevated my stress level and impacted my ability to regulate my own reactions.*

*I paused, agreed with the student, and used the opportunity to help the class take a breath with me. We took three collective breaths and did a few calming yoga exercises to regulate our collective physical experiences. This simple pause helped reset the tone so we could continue the classroom instruction and get learning back on track for everyone.*

## STAR Method

One way to do a quick nonverbal communication self-check is to use the **STAR method.** The STAR method focuses on four key ways to engage with a speaker:

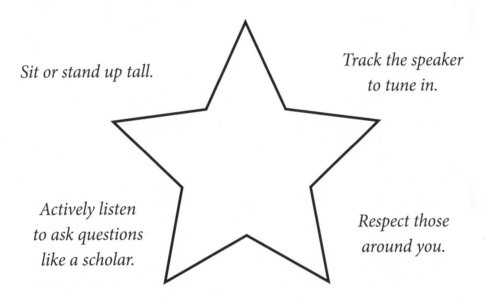

*Sit or stand up tall.*

*Track the speaker to tune in.*

*Actively listen to ask questions like a scholar.*

*Respect those around you.*

**Sit or stand up tall.** If the porcupine is sitting, get down to their eye level and sit up tall while they share their concerns with you. Rest your hands in a place that feels comfortable to you; anchor both heels (or hip bones, if seated directly on the floor) into the ground; and square your shoulders in the direction of the porcupine. If the porcupine is standing, then stand at their eye level with both heels equally anchored into the ground. Rest your hands comfortably at your side while your porcupine speaks.

**Track the speaker to tune in.** Physically follow the speaker with your eyes and torso. This means squaring your hips or shoulders in the direction of the speaker and making direct eye contact when appropriate. Interpret the porcupine's nonverbals and mirror the calmer expressions. If appropriate, take notes to demonstrate you are listening and following their experience.

**Actively listen to ask questions like a scholar.** Identify the porcupine's underlying needs or emotions by tracking their nonverbal body language. Then ask questions that help the porcupine better articulate their needs. Doing so structures the conversation to help the porcupine identify a potential solution or resolution.

**Respect those around you.** Everything we do as youth workers must be done with respect for those around us. Actively listen to the porcupine and consider respectful ways to resolve the situation. I like using a strengths-based approach that assumes positive intent and focuses on the youth's positive qualities as a baseline. This strategy helps ground the conversation and focus on the youth's lived experience at present while funneling out initial biases that can cloud our perceptions or assumptions.

## TAKE ACTION: STAR METHOD

*Write your answers here or in appendix 1, section 3.*

Take a moment to practice the following nonverbals. Notice how you feel. Then describe your thoughts and feelings in writing.

    1. Sit or stand tall.

2. Track the movements of the next person who speaks to or with you to tune in.

3. Actively listen and ask strategic and engaging questions of the next person who interacts with you. Did you learn anything new or different?

4. Respect every person as an individual. Approach your next prickly interaction by assuming positive intent.

## Practice and Reflect

De-escalating and effectively engaging with porcupines is all about forming a relationship and building a plan unique to the youth in that relationship. The ARISE methodology is designed to provide you with tools you can swap out based on the unique needs of the porcupine. Mix and match elements of ARISE to create appropriate responses for each moment.

We all start in different places with different results. Strong, reliable, well-equipped communication tool kits are built up over time. The porcupines you meet today are different from the porcupines you met yesterday and the porcupines you will meet next year. Likewise, your communication tactics may not be the same either. As such, it is essential you practice, practice, practice! Practice identifying, interpreting, and employing effective verbal and nonverbal communication strategies to help de-escalate prickly porcupines.

You have taken important steps to build out a framework for communicating with porcupines. Keep up the momentum by regularly checking in and revisiting your plan. Add in or swap out communication activities or tricks as you become proficient. Improving your communication skills is a lifelong journey.

# TAKE ACTION: START YOUR JOURNEY

*Use the goal-setting form in appendix 3 to build on your current skill set.*

## Set Your Goal

Think about why you are here. What do you want to get better at doing? Where do you think you can improve your communication?

Specific: What do I want to do?

**Measurable:** How will I track my progress?

**Achievable:** Is this realistic for me?

**Results-focused** or **Reasonable:** Why am I doing this?

**Time-limited:** When will I have this completed?

**Set your goal:** I will _____ by _____.

## Reflect on Next Steps

Now that you have your goal, consider the following, and write down your responses:

What steps do you need to take to get there?

What can you start doing today?

Post your goal in a place where you will see it daily. An unwritten goal is just a dream.

## Gather Feedback

*Use the guided Communication Interview in appendix 4.*
Now that you've completed your ARISE action plan and taken many notes along the way, it's time to gather feedback from a friend, family member, or coworker. Select a trusted person to observe and react to your communication approach.

## Build Momentum

Schedule time to revisit your action plan—quarterly, biannually, or annually. You pick the cadence that works for you. If you use a paper calendar, pencil in a few days this month to revisit your action plan. If you use an electronic calendar, set up a recurring reminder.

# Conclusion

I wrote this field guide to help you

- learn how to identify porcupines,
- broaden your communication know-how to skillfully handle prickly people and situations, and
- implement your own action plan for redirecting and de-escalating porcupines.

I designed this guide for youth workers like you, who encounter prickly porcupines in the field. I hope you found it an informative and practical resource to which you can refer over and over throughout your career.

Take a moment to reflect on all you've read, applied, and learned while navigating this field guide. Are you confident you can effectively identify a porcupine? Will you ARISE to the porcupine's needs? Will you better train your colleagues in ways to verbally de-escalate a porcupine? Do you feel better equipped to be a more effective youth worker? Will you practice more communication techniques in your leadership role?

I hope so.

•••••••

I love hearing from youth workers. Please share how you're doing in your own communication practice. Send me a note at howtotalktoporcupines@gmail.com or visit me at howtotalktoporcupines.com. Also feel free to follow me on any of the platforms below:

- Instagram: @howtotalktoporcupines
- Facebook: @howtotalktoporcupines
- LinkedIn: linkedin.com/company/howtotalktoporcupines

Use **#HowtoTalktoPorcupines** in your social media posts and show me what you're doing to support youth today.

## NOTE

If you made it this far and are disheartened because I did not teach you the actual language of real-life porcupines, my sincerest apologies. I recommend you search for "Teddy Bear the Porcupine" online. You just might find the fun, chatty rodent you're looking for!

# Acknowledgments

This field guide took a village to bring to life. While you may not be named here, know I am thankful beyond words for your support.

I would not be here without my spouse, who put the bug in my ear late one night with a simple question: "Have you considered making this professional development workshop into a book?" I reacted as most prickly personalities react to questions they deem silly . . . by turning off the light and pulling the blankets over my head. Yet my spouse championed the idea, and it took off.

To my spouse, thank you. This book would not have happened without your simple question, and I appreciate your support when I disappeared into my computer for hours on end.

To my immediate and extended family, thank you for proofreading early versions of the manuscript and sharing your own porcupine moments with me. I am especially grateful to my friends and family members who, while writing their own books, made space to read my manuscript and provide constructive feedback and professional guidance.

I owe all the porcupine design and early branding genius to AKimball Creative, who was attuned to the iconography after a few short discussions and well before I truly understood what the porcupine visual needed to be. Thank you to Beaver's Pond Press for taking these designs further and incorporating them into this field guide. I am also grateful for the time and energy allocated by my robust editing team, which helped create a crisper message.

Thank you to the staff at Youth Intervention Programs Association (YIPA) for encouraging me over the years by giving me space to learn from incredible youth workers as well as present my own work at events. Without your support and tireless advocacy for youth workers, the seed for *How to Talk to Porcupines* may not have been planted.

Thank you to the leaders in my life who quite literally dropped undaunted hints to push me further into my full potential at just the right time.

Finally, thank you to those whose stories and mentorship provided me with the inspiration and experience to quickly recognize and respond to prickly situations. As mentors, teachers, and educators in my life, you taught me so much when I was a prickly youth and an adult learner. Your incredible wisdom influenced many strategies featured in this guide.

# Appendix 1: Field Guide Workbook

## SECTION 1: PRICKLY PERSONALITIES

**Bristly Behavior**

Porcupines demonstrate warning behaviors to predators. What behaviors do youth demonstrate when threatened, fearful, or concerned for their safety?

**Identify Your Porcupines**

Describe the porcupines in your life.

When do you typically see porcupines? Consider time of day, location, environment, activity, and subject matter.

Which prickly porcupine attributes or behaviors do you most frequently encounter?

How do you feel when you encounter a prickly personality?

# SECTION 2: CHATTER CATAGORIES

### Dress Effect
Search for the "dress illusion" online. What color(s) do you see?

### Perspectives
When have perspectives caused a miscommunication in your work? What was the result?

**Perceptions**

It is important to be aware of in-group bias perceptions as a youth worker.

What in-group biases might you hold?

How do your in-group biases impact the way you perceive the youth with whom you work?

Could your in-group biases impact the way you communicate with youth? How?

**Assumptions**
When have assumptions caused a communication breakdown in your work?
What was the result?

How long do you allow youth to speak or share their story before interrupting?

**Objectives**

In what ways have differing objectives caused communication breakdown in your work?

**Emotions**

What emotions do you see most frequently in youth attending your program?

How do these emotions impact or influence communication in your program?

Consider your own emotions. What raises your quills, aggravates you, or pushes your buttons?

When your quills are up, how does it impact your relationship with youth?

**Styles**

What kinds of communication styles have you encountered in your role as a youth worker?

# SECTION 3: PORCUPINE PLANS

**Audit and Explore**

_Reflect on Communication Divides_

Take a moment to honestly reflect on your communication with prickly personalities. What does it feel like to encounter a prickly personality?

How comfortable are you engaging with a prickly personality?

Describe how you feel when you have successfully redirected or de-escalated a prickly personality.

### *Name a Porcupine*

The first step in your action plan is to identify a porcupine. Who is the prickly porcupine you want to assist? Where do you encounter this porcupine? How old are they?

This porcupine is _____.

I encounter this porcupine in _____.

This porcupine is about _____ years old.

**Actively Listen**

Practice staying present with meditation.

1. Find a relaxing position seated or lying down in a quiet space.

2. Start to focus on your breath, breathing in for a count of four and out for a count of four. Pause between breaths.

3. Notice tension drip away from your jaw. Let your neck and shoulders relax.

4. Allow your elbows to release and fingers to fall away from your body.

5. Notice any tension in your hips—let it go.

6. Allow your knees and ankles to release.

7. Try to clear your mind of any thoughts. If a thought enters, notice it, acknowledge it, and let it go. Stay here for as long as is comfortable, letting your thoughts fall away.

Reflect on your meditative experience here.

**Actively Listen**

Write down three ways to practice active listening today.

1.

2.

3.

## Targeted Questions

Write down three open-ended questions you already use.

1.

2.

3.

Write down three open-ended questions you want to start using.

1.

2.

3.

Write down three close-ended questions you already use.

1.

2.

3.

Write down three close-ended questions you want to start using.

1.

2.

3.

**Minimal Encourages**
Write down three minimal encourages you can start using today.

1.

2.

3.

**Include Voices**
In what ways does your organization bring the voice of the youth you serve to the table?

What questions or tactics can you use to include others in the conversation? Write them down.

1.

2.

3.

4.

5.

6.

**Inclusive Alternatives**

*Leverage Inclusive Language and Replace Exclusive Language*

Which words would you add to this table? Write them on a separate sheet of paper or fill in the empty boxes.

| Exclusive Term | Inclusive Alternative |
| --- | --- |
| bossy | leader, organizer |
| disabled person | person who lives with a disability or exceptionality |
| ghetto | neighborhood, enclave, home, locality, place |
| guys/gals | folks, folx, y'all |
| handicap | disability, exceptionality |
| lame | boring, lackluster, unimpressive |
| man (e.g., manpower) | human, people |
| underrepresented | marginalized, excluded, disenfranchised |
|  |  |
|  |  |
|  |  |

**Clearly Explain**

How might you restate a rule to easily explain its importance in your program? Write out a restatement now:

**Demonstrate Empathy**

Write three empathy-based questions you can use to establish rapport with youth in your program.

1.

2.

3.

**Bounce-Back Statements**

Rewrite the statements below as bounce-back statements:

1. You stopped writing.

2. You made a mess.

3. Stop running around the pool.

4. Stop picking your nose.

5. You didn't wash your hands before eating.

Now write your own bounce-back statements. Consider statements you can use with your youth today.

1.

2.

3.

**STAR Method**

Take a moment to practice the following nonverbals. Notice how you feel. Then, describe your thoughts and feelings here.

1. Sit or stand tall.

2. Track the movements of the next person who speaks to or with you to tune in.

3. Actively listen and ask strategic and engaging questions of the next person who interacts with you. Did you learn anything new or different?

4. Respect every person as an individual. Approach your next prickly interaction by assuming positive intent.

# Appendix 2:
# "Yes, and . . ." Activity

Find a partner. This could be a trusted coworker, family member, or close friend. Decide which of you will be Person A and which will be Person B.

**Round 1**

Person A always states a declaration.

Person B always replies with a declaration beginning with the word "But . . ."

Let's look at an example:

    Person A: I'm going on a trip, and I'm bringing my dog.

    Person B: But your dog shouldn't be cooped up that long.

    Person A: I'm going on a trip, and I'm bringing my favorite suitcase.

    Person B: But your suitcase is too small.

    Person A: I'm going on a trip, and I'm bringing my friend.

    Person B: But what about your family?

    Person A: I'm going on a trip and . . .

    Person B: But . . .

**Pause and reflect.** How did this conversation make you feel? (Circle your answer.)

    Person A: After this conversation, I felt     empowered    defeated

    Person B: After this conversation, I felt     empowered    defeated

Did Person A and B share similar emotions or feelings? Write your thoughts below.

## Round 2

Repeat the same exercise with one edit. This time, Person B always replies with a declaration beginning with the phrase "Yes, and . . ."

Let's take a look:

Person A: I'm going on a trip, and I'm bringing my favorite suitcase.

Person B: Yes, and your suitcase is perfect for your beach clothes!

Person A: I'm going on a trip, and I'm bringing my friend.

Person B: Yes, and your friend is going to have a great time!

Person A: I'm going on a trip, and I'm bringing sunscreen.

Person B: Yes, and you are so smart!

Person A: I'm going on a trip, and . . .

Person B: Yes, and . . .

**Pause and reflect.** How did this conversation make you feel?

Person A: After this conversation, I felt          empowered          defeated

Person B: After this conversation, I felt          empowered          defeated

Did Person A and Person B share similar emotions or feelings?
Write your thoughts below.

Which round left you feeling defeated? Why?

Which round left you feeling empowered? Why?

# Appendix 3:
# Start Your Journey

## *Set Your Goal*

Consider the principles of communication presented in the ARISE model. What would you like to add to your communication tool kit? What would you like to work on?

**Take a moment to determine your communication goal by completing the table below:**

| | |
|---|---|
| Specific | What exactly do I want to do? |
| Measurable | How will I track my progress? |
| Achievable | Is this realistic for me? |
| Results-focused or Reasonable | Why am I doing this? |
| Time-limited | When will I have this completed? |

**Set your goal:** I will_____ by _____.

*Reflect on Next Steps*

**Now that you have your goal, consider the following:**

What steps do you need to take to get there?

What can you  start doing today?

Post your goal in a place where you will see it daily. An unwritten goal is just a dream.

*Build Momentum*

Schedule time to revisit your action plan—quarterly, biannually, or annually. You pick the cadence that works for you. If you use a paper calendar, pencil in a few days this month to revisit your action plan. If you use an electronic calendar, set up a recurring reminder.

# Appendix 4: Communication Interview

**Remember: You asked for feedback. Do not try to explain, argue, justify, or otherwise undermine the answers you receive. Just listen and reflect.**

Circle the descriptor(s) that apply to your relationship with the person you are interviewing:

Personal          Professional          Family

Other: _____

1. In what ways do we communicate (e.g., emails, text messages, face-to-face, meetings, trainings/presentations)?

2. Describe the setting where we communicate most frequently.

3. What communication challenges do you see in this setting?

4. What makes a strong communicator in this setting? What makes a weak communicator in this setting?

5. How do you see me use _____ in everyday communication *(Select one of the ARISE communication? principles.)*

Ask your communication interview partner to conduct an observation of your communication skills using the following tables and corresponding questions.

Conduct an observation of no fewer than ten minutes and place a check mark in the appropriate box when the respective behavior is observed.

**Observation date:** _____

**Observation location:** _____

## Level of observation

| Behavior demonstrated | | Not observed | Rarely uses | Sometimes uses | Always uses |
|---|---|---|---|---|---|
| **Actively Listen** | Listens to and values others' ideas | | | | |
| | Listens to the full story before responding | | | | |
| | Uses empathy-based listening to uncover the speaker's needs | | | | |
| | Spends more time listening than talking | | | | |
| | Demonstrates generic, unintrusive conversational cues to encourage the speaker to continue | | | | |
| **Total:** | | | | | |

## Level of observation

| Behavior demonstrated | Not observed | Rarely uses | Sometimes uses | Always uses |
|---|---|---|---|---|
| **Respond Appropriately** — Establishes rapport | | | | |
| Leverages a variety of question types to uncover the speaker's point of view | | | | |
| Demonstrates respect for others in responses | | | | |
| Adjusts responses to meet the unique needs of the speaker | | | | |
| Uses affect labeling to assist the speaker in identifying their emotion(s) | | | | |
| | | | | |
| **Total:** | | | | |

## Level of observation

| Behavior demonstrated | Not observed | Rarely uses | Sometimes uses | Always uses |
|---|---|---|---|---|
| Collaborates to ensure the speaker's needs are met | | | | |
| Leverages inclusive language | | | | |
| Employs input panels to gather multiple avenues of information or feedback | | | | |
| Actively draws all members of the program into the activity or conversation | | | | |
| Recognizes personal and professional limits | | | | |
| Demonstrates willingness to set aside ego to resolve conflict | | | | |
| | | | | |
| Total: | | | | |

**Include Voices**

## Level of observation

| Behavior demonstrated | Not observed | Rarely uses | Sometimes uses | Always uses |
|---|---|---|---|---|
| **Structure** Builds on the speaker's experience and knowledge to navigate a conversation or conflict | | | | |
| Introduces the plan before jumping in | | | | |
| Explains the reason for the activity or direction | | | | |
| Remains clear and concise | | | | |
| Engages the speaker with bounce-back statements | | | | |
| | | | | |
| **Total:** | | | | |

## Level of observation

| Behavior demonstrated | Not observed | Rarely uses | Sometimes uses | Always uses |
|---|---|---|---|---|
| **Employ Nonverbals** — Uses wait time effectively | | | | |
| Communicates on the same eye level as the speaker | | | | |
| Sets aside all distractions while engaging with the speaker | | | | |
| Notices physical distance from the speaker or placement between the speaker and exit | | | | |
| Manages facial expressions appropriately | | | | |
| Physically tracks the speaker to tune in | | | | |
| **Total:** | | | | |

1. Describe the setting where this observation took place.

2. What patterns emerge in the tables?

3. What are three things you think I could work on to become a better communicator?

4. Who else would you recommend I speak with to help me become a stronger communicator?

# Glossary

**#HowtoTalktoPorcupines.** A hashtag to join the chatter and connect with like-minded youth workers on social media.

**active listening.** A technique that demonstrates approachability and availability in communication. Compare *empathy-based listening*; see also *minimal encourage*.

**affect labeling.** The practice of identifying the primary emotion behind words.

**aggressive communicator.** An individual who expresses their ideas strongly and may demand, command, or leverage sarcasm, often at the expense of others. See also *communication*; compare *passive-aggressive communicator*.

**ARISE.** An abbreviation for *Actively listen; Respond appropriately; Include Voices; Structure; and Employ nonverbals.* A communication tool designed to effectively plan for, redirect, and de-escalate porcupine moments.

**assumption.** A statement accepted to be true without proof.

**bounce-back statement.** A tool used to structure conversations toward resolution by describing expected behavior in a positive light, empowering the listener to try again.

**close-ended question.** A question used to close a deal or agree on next steps. It is typically designed to elicit a dichotomy response in which there are only two options: yes or no. Contrast *open-ended question*; see also *targeted questioning*.

**communication.** The way in which people send and receive messages. Breakdown occurs when a message is interrupted, incorrectly transmitted, incorrectly received, or misunderstood. *Nonverbal communication* recognizes the transmission of messages that do not involve words or vocal components (e.g., body language, positioning, and clothing). *Verbal communication* recognizes the selection of words used to convey or share ideas, messages, or needs with others.

*Vocal communication* recognizes the tone, register, volume, and resonance with which we project our voices as we share ideas, messages, or needs with others.

**direct communicator.** An individual who focuses on the intent of their message by cutting away fluff and delivering succinct statements. Contrast *indirect communicator*; see also *communication*.

**direct miscommunication.** A type of communication breakdown that occurs when a youth tells an explicit lie. Contrast *indirect miscommunication*; see also *communication*.

**emotion.** A state of feeling that influences the way people process or receive information. Examples include sadness, loss, grief, anxiety, stress, fear, happiness, excitement, and contentedness. See also *affect labeling*; *emotional intelligence*.

**emotional intelligence.** The act of perceiving emotions, understanding emotions, regulating emotions in oneself or others, and using emotions to facilitate cognitive activities.

**empathy-based listening.** The practice of seeking to understand and validate the porcupine's unique experiences. Compare *active listening*.

**indirect communicator.** An individual who expresses themselves with ambiguity, using nuances, metaphors, or small talk to introduce their intended message. Contrast *direct communicator*; see also *communication*.

**indirect miscommunication.** A type of communication breakdown that occurs when youth workers miss or misunderstand key aspects of the youth's story. Contrast *direct miscommunication*; see also *communication*.

**in-group bias.** The automatic tendency (whether consciously or unconsciously) to show preference for people who share certain commonalities with us.

**instructional structuring.** See also *scaffolding*.

**learning brain.** A regulated brain space in which individuals process small changes and new information with relative ease. Contrast *survival brain*.

**manipulative communicator.** An individual who leverages a variety of communication tools to express their ideas in a way designed to make the other party feel sorry or guilty enough to take action.

**minimal encourage.** A listener strategy used to empower the speaker to carry on with their story. These include small verbal or nonverbal responses designed to nudge the speaker to keep talking.

**nonverbal communication.** See *communication.*

**objective.** The goal or reason for communicating.

**open-ended question.** A question used to make people feel important or understand a point of view. Contrast *close-ended question;* see also *targeted questioning.*

**passive-aggressive communicator.** An individual who controls conversations with statements designed to sound supportive while simultaneously cutting others down. Compare *aggressive communicator.*

**perception.** The means in which we understand or interpret a situation through our observations, thoughts, beliefs, attribution, identity, or judgement. See also *in-group bias; perspective.*

**perspective.** A vantage point from which we approach experiences and communication, often deriving from our varying levels of background information, situational awareness, point of view, and attitude. See also *perception.*

**porcupine.** An individual who feels threatened or challenged and is engaging in angry, regressive conversation; experiencing a power imbalance; miscommunicating directly or indirectly; withdrawing from the discussion; or navigating a difficult conversation.

**scaffolding.** Also called *instructional structuring.* A methodology that occurs when an educator builds on a student's experiences and knowledge to enhance their learning and aid in the mastery of tasks. It is comprised of the following steps: introduce what you plan to discuss before jumping in; explain the reason for what you are saying as you say it; be clear and concise; empathize; agree and take action.

**STAR.** An abbreviation for *Sit or stand up tall; Track the speaker to tune in; Actively listen to ask questions like a scholar; and Respect those around you.* A method designed to help you do a quick nonverbal communication self-check. See also *communication.*

**strategic question.** An open-ended question asked with a targeted purpose, often intended to maximize the likelihood of getting a porcupine to say yes by placing the power in their hands. See also *open-ended question; targeted questioning.*

**style.** The unique way individuals communicate as influenced by community, region, culture, age, and industry. See also *perception; perspective.*

**survival brain.** A hyper-focused state in which the brain cannot process complex reasoning. Contrast *learning brain.*

**targeted questioning.** A strategy to move conversation forward through a combination of open- and close-ended questions.

**verbal communication.** See *communication.*

**vocal communication.** See *communication.*

**wait time.** A purposeful pause to provide a porcupine space to process and respond to a question, comment, or instruction.

***"Yes, and"* statement.** A technique that uses inclusive language to build on the experience and truth of the speaker by saying, "Yes, and . . ." in response to the speaker's comments.

# References

Beckman, Howard B., and Richard M. Frankel. 1984. "The Effect of Physician Behavior on Collection of Date." *Annals of Internal Medicine* 101, no. 5 (December): 692–96. https://doi.org/10.7326/0003-4819-101-5-692.

Benas, Nick, and Michele Hart. 2017. *Mental Health Emergencies: A First-Responder's Guide to Recognizing and Handling Mental Health Crises.* Hobart, NY: Hatherleigh Press.

Bonet, Diana. 1994. *The Business of Listening: A Practical Guide to Effective Listening.* Rev. ed. Menlo Park, CA: Crisp Publications.

Csikszentmihalyi, Mihaly, and Reed Larson. 1984. *Being Adolescent: Conflict and Growth in the Teenage Years.* New York: Basic Books.

Hartley, Gregory, and Maryann Karinch. 2017. *The Art of Body Talk: How to Decode Gestures, Mannerisms, and Other Non-verbal Messages.* Wayne, NJ: Career Press.

Li, Han Z., Michael Krysko, Naghmeh G. Desroches, and George Deagle. 2004. "Reconceptualizing Interruptions in Physician–Patient Interviews: Cooperative and Intrusive." *Communication & Medicine* 1, no. 2: 145–57. https://doi.org/10.1515/come.2004.1.2.145.

Marvel, M. Kim, Ronald M. Epstein, Kristine Flowers, and Howard B. Beckman. 1999. "Soliciting the Patient's Agenda: Have We Improved?" *JAMA* 281, no. 3 (January): 283–87. https://doi.org/10.1001/jama.281.3.283.

Mehrabian, Albert, and Morton Wiener. 1967. "Decoding of Inconsistent Communications." *Journal of Personality and Social Psychology* 6, no. 1: 109–14. https://doi.org/10.1037/h0024532.

Meunier, Paul, host. The Passionate Youth Worker (podcast). https://training.yipa.org/podcast.

Murphy, Linda K. 2020. *Declarative Language Handbook: Using a Thoughtful Language Style to Help Kids with Social Learning Challenges Feel Competent, Connected, and Understood.* N.p.

Noll, Douglas E. 2017. *De-escalate: How to Calm an Angry Person in 90 Seconds or Less.* New York: Atria PaperBooks.

Ofri, Danielle. 2017. *What Patients Say, What Doctors Hear: What Doctors Say, What Patients Hear.* Boston: Beacon Press.

Puiman, Rosalie. 2019. *The Mindful Guide to Conflict Resolution: How to Thoughtfully Handle Difficult Situations, Conversations, and Personalities.* New York: Adams Media.

Rogers, Adam. 2015. "The Science of Why No One Agrees on the Color of This Dress." *Wired*, February 26, 2015. https://www.wired.com/2015/02/science-one-agrees-color-dress.

Salovey, Peter, John D. Mayer, David Caruso, and Seung Hee Yoo. 2009. "The Positive Psychology of Emotional Intelligence." In *The Oxford Handbook of Positive Psychology*, 2nd ed., edited by Shane J. Lopez and C.R. Snyder, 237–48. New York: Oxford University Press.

Schaenen, Inda. 2014. *Speaking of Fourth Grade: What Listening to Kids Tells Us about School in America.* New York: The New Press.

Singh Ospina, Naykky, Kari A. Phillips, Rene Rodriguez-Gutierrez, Ana Castaneda-Guarderas, Michael R. Gionfriddo, Megan E. Branda, and Victor M. Montori. 2019. "Eliciting the Patient's Agenda- Secondary Analysis of Recorded Clinical Encounters." *Journal of General Internal Medicine* 34: 36–40. https://doi.org/10.1007/s11606-018-4540-5.

Treasure, Julian. 2013. "How to Speak So That People Want to Listen." Filmed June 2013 at TedXGlobal in Edinburgh, Scotland. Video, 9:45. https://www.ted.com/talks/julian_treasure_how_to_speak_so_that_people_want_to_listen.

Van Slyke, Erik J. 1999. *Listening to Conflict: Finding Constructive Solutions to Workplace Disputes.* New York: AMACOM.

Van Vugt, Mark, and Mark Schaller. 2008. "Evolutionary Approaches to Group Dynamics: An Introduction." *Group Dynamics: Theory, Research, and Practice*, 12, no. 1: 1–6. https://doi.org/10.1037/1089-2699.12.1.1.

Wallisch, Pascal. 2017. "Illumination Assumptions Account for Individual Differences in the Perceptual Interpretation of a Profoundly Ambiguous Stimulus in the Color Domain: 'The Dress.'" *Journal of Vision* 17, no. 4. https://doi.org/10.1167/17.4.5.

# Index

Allegra Birdseye-Hannula is a lifelong learner and a youth worker, learning and development specialist, and public speaker by trade. She is passionate about delivering impactful communication and de-escalation strategies to help youth workers address the needs of prickly youth. For more information about Allegra's work, visit howtotalktoporcupines.com.

In her free time, Allegra enjoys local parks; savoring a cup of coffee or tea; cross-country skiing; making music (drums, marimba, and piano); or sketching and painting.